ETHNOGRAPHIC DECISION TREE MODELING

CHRISTINA H. GLADWIN
University of Florida

Qualitative Research Methods
Volume 19

SAGE PUBLICATIONS
The Publishers of Professional Social Science
Newbury Park   London   New Delhi

For information address:

SAGE Publications, Inc.
2111 West Hillcrest Drive
Newbury Park, California 91320

SAGE Publications Ltd.
28 Banner Street
London EC1Y 8QE
England

SAGE Publications India Pvt. Ltd.
M-32 Market
Greater Kailash I
New Delhi 110 048 India

Printed in the United States of America
Library of Congress Cataloging-in-Publication Data

Gladwin, Christina H.
    Ethnographic decision tree modeling / by Christina H. Gladwin.
        p. cm. — (Qualitative research methods ; 19)
    Bibliography: p.
    ISBN 0-8039-3486-6. — ISBN 0-8039-3487-4 (pbk.)
    1. Ethnology — Methodology. I. Title. II. Series: Qualitative research methods ; v. 19.
    GN345.G55   1989
306′.01 — dc20   89-10523
                                                                CIP

SBEN 2993IP 8-5-2013
FIRST PRINTING, 1989

When citing a University Paper, please use the proper form. Remember to cite the correct Sage University Paper series title and include the paper number. One of the following formats can be adapted (depending on the style manual used):

(1) KIRK, JEROME and MARC L. MILLER (1986) Reliability and Validity in Qualitative Research. Sage University Paper Series on Qualitative Research Methods, Vol. 1. Beverly Hills, CA: Sage.

or

(2) Kirk, J., & Miller, M. L. (1986). *Reliability and validity in qualitative research* (Sage University Paper Series on Qualitative Research Methods, Vol. 1). Beverly Hills, CA: Sage.

CONTENTS

This monograph is dedicated to my role model and mother, Rose Horn. I am grateful for her support, her love of learning for its own sake, her discipline, and the time she took to teach me things. I am thankful for the long-term encouragement of Hugh, Mark, and Amy Gladwin, Ossie Werner, Russ Bernard, and Bert Pelto, for students who have demanded a text, including those of the National Science Foundation's Anthropology Summer Methods Institute, 1987 and 1988, and for sympathetic and constructive reviews from Michael Burton, Susan Weller, Marc Miller, and John Van Maanen. Finally, I am grateful to my department, Food and Resource Economics, University of Florida, for giving me time to write. Naturally, I take full responsibility for all ideas expressed herein.

EDITOR'S INTRODUCTION

One of the enduring and thorny riddles of social behavior has to do with why people act as they do. When speaking teleologically about motives, common experience suggests that behavior is often the planned consequence of rather carefully considered choices. Indeed, assumptions about the strong influence of reason on everyday action are standard in the social sciences. A major problem, of course, is that empirical procedures for documenting — much less predicting — what and how people think have been slow to evolve. This situation is profoundly remedied by Christina H. Gladwin's *Ethnographic Decision Tree Modeling*, Volume 19 of Sage's *Qualitative Research Methods Series*.

Gladwin's basic argument is straightforward and appealing. First, she notes that people have the ability to report on real-life decisions in terms of alternatives evaluated, dimensions of contrast (and their relative weights), and sequencing of comparisons. Second, Gladwin rightly sees ethnography as uniquely suited for the elicitation of contextual information about decisions. Third, she finds scientific research design and logic appropriate to the jobs of sampling subjects, developing hypotheses, and designing descriptive and, ultimately, predictive models of decision making. With this understanding — and drawing illustrations from groups as different as American university students and African farmers — Gladwin tells us exactly how to (and how not to) build, test, and refine hierarchical models of the simple, nested, and composite kinds.

This book is an especially welcome addition to the *Series* because it underscores the value of a wide range of ethnographic techniques (concerning, for example, strategies for interviewing, questionnaire design, and achieving rapport) to scientific inquiry. Gladwin's insights about ways to study the role of cognition in shaping choice are certain to improve the quality of abstract and applied qualitative research.

Marc L. Miller
Peter K. Manning
John Van Maanen

Why vs. what?

ETHNOGRAPHIC DECISION TREE MODELING

CHRISTINA GLADWIN
University of Florida

1. WHY MODEL HOW PEOPLE MAKE DECISIONS?

Psychologists at a drug rehabilitation center want to know how kids decide what drugs to use, and how they decide to switch from soft to hard drugs. Educators want to know why university enrollment by Blacks is decreasing in the 1980s. Sociologists in a women's studies center want to know why women's groups disband so frequently. Agricultural experts in the Third World want to know why farmers are not adopting the improved technologies coming out of their research stations and "on-farm" trials. Environmentalists want to know why forests and marine fisheries are being depleted. Economists in sub-Saharan Africa want to know if African farmers will still use chemical fertilizers when the fertilizer subsidy (and price distortion) is removed. Social workers in the inner cities of the United States want to know why teenage pregnancies are on the rise.

What do all these people have in common? They want to know why people in a certain group do what they do. They need to know how these people make a real-world decision, and they need to know the specific decision criteria used by the group in question, in case they can intervene in the decision-making process with a new policy designed to make things better. They are not so interested in theorizing about the choice process itself, or even in knowing how a particular individual makes a decision, but are concerned with predicting *group* rather than

7

individual behavior. Yet, they realize decision making is most frequently an individualized enterprise, although groups of people in meetings and individuals on their own both make decisions. However, because they want to predict group behavior in situations in which it is *individuals* who are making the decisions, they want a social scientist to tell them *why* most of the individuals in the group make the choices they do.

The purpose of this monograph is to describe a methodology – a qualitative method – to do just that. The method has been used during the past two decades by ethnographers in many cultures to predict the actual choices of individuals in a group. Decision trees have predicted, with a high degree of accuracy in a wide variety of choice contexts, a great number of decisions. These include decisions made by Ghanaian fish sellers in deciding between markets (H. Gladwin, 1971; C. Gladwin, 1975; Quinn, 1978), farmers' adoption decisions in Puebla, Mexico (C. Gladwin, 1976, 1977, 1979a, 1979b), Californian families' decisions regarding the sexual division of labor within the family for daily routine tasks (Mukhopadhyay, 1984), farmers' cropping decisions (Barlett, 1977; C. Gladwin, 1983), peasants' choice of treatment for illness in Pichatero, Mexico (Young, 1980, 1981), United States car buyers' choice of cars (H. Gladwin and Murtaugh, 1980, 1984), economic development decisions of the Navajo tribe (Schoepfle, Burton and Morgan, 1984), and United States farmers' decisions to cut back production and sell land during a farm crisis (Zabawa, 1984; C. Gladwin and Zabawa, 1984, 1986, 1987). In each case in which the method has been used, the predictability has been as high as 85 to 95% of the historical choice data used to test the model. These success rates are remarkable, however, only because most studies of economic decision making do not test the model against choice data collected from more than one individual (Anderson, 1979; Anderson, Dillon and Hardaker, 1977; Benito, 1976; Moscardi and deJanvry, 1977; Roy, 1952; Roumasset, 1976; Roumasset, Boussard and Singh, 1979).

The method is called *ethnographic decision tree modeling* because it uses ethnographic fieldwork techniques to elicit from the decision makers themselves their decision criteria, which are then combined in the form of a *decision tree, table, flowchart,* or *set of "if-then rules"* or *"expert systems"* which can be programmed on the computer. There are thus two distinctive features about the method, which are discussed in turn below: its reliance on ethnographic fieldwork techniques to elicit the decision criteria, and its insistence on a formal, testable, computer-based model of the decision process which is *hierarchical* or treelike in nature.

To See the Insiders' World Through the Insiders' Eyes

Ethnographic decision tree modeling starts from the assumption that the decision makers themselves are the experts on how they make the decisions they make. It uses ethnographic techniques developed by anthropologists — ethnographers — to elicit the specific decision criteria used by the decision makers when making a real-world decision. Ethnography is the work of describing a culture from the "native's" or *insider's* point of view and not from the researcher's or *outsider's* point of view; it is accomplished through field techniques like "the ethnographic interview" (Spradley, 1979) and "participation observation" (Spradley, 1980). To minimize the researcher's own ethnocentricity, i.e., the viewing of another culture through the lens of one's own cultural values and assumptions, the ethnographer seeks to learn from people, to be taught by them like a child is taught. The aim is to discover the cultural meaning of the insiders' relationships, native terms, rules, and way of life (Spradley, 1979: 3). Discovering the insider's world from the insider's point of view is a far different goal from that of collecting data about people and testing a model based on the outsider's view. Decision criteria should thus contain "emic" categories, i.e., units of meaning drawn from the culture bearers themselves, which can be contrasted with "etic" categories, which may have meaning for researchers but need not have meaning for the people of the specific culture under study (Pike, 1954; Harris, 1979: 32-45).

Analogously, ethnographic decision tree modeling is *not* a black-box technique to test the researcher's interpretation of the insiders' culture, like some quantitative methods (e.g., factor analysis, multidimensional scaling, cluster analysis). Instead, it is a way to build a computer-based or *expert-systems* model of the insiders' decision processes from the insiders' own terms and phrasing of their decision criteria. Because of this dependence on eliciting procedures to elicit the rules and emic categories to build the model, ethnographic decision tree models differ from other expert systems or rule-based models which are less context-sensitive. With the ethnographic approach, the model is culturally tuned by some specific group of individuals and then tested against choice data from other individuals in the group. Decision tree models are also similar to other ethnographic techniques or cognitive-science models like taxonomies, componential analysis, and plans or scripts, described in detail elsewhere (Schank and Abelson, 1979; Werner and Schoepfle, 1987). They are thus an outgrowth of the "cognitive revolution" that has taken the disciplines of anthropology, psychology, linguistics, artificial intelligence, neuroscience, and philosophy by storm since 1956 (Gardner, 1985).

A Treelike Formal Model

Decision tree methodology assumes that, on the one hand, verbal descriptions of native actors' decision criteria, such as are found in some excellent ethnographies (Cancian, 1972), are not enough. Formal models and testing procedures are necessary. To minimize the researcher's own ethnocentrism when specifying decision criteria and building a decision model, a test of his or her hypotheses about how native actors make their decisions should be designed and empirical choice data collected to make the test.

On the other hand, the methodology assumes that the traditional quantitative decision models which are linear-additive models and often normative (e.g., linear programming models, expected-value and expected-utility models, stochastic-dominance models) are also not sufficient because, typically, they are not empirically grounded. They are not usually tested against a set of choice data to see how well they predict the choices of individuals in a group (see Anderson, 1979; Anderson, Dillon and Hardaker, 1977). Instead, they are used either as behavioral assumptions in a model of aggregate supply or demand or as normative models to tell people how they *should* make decisions (Raiffa, 1968), or they are tested to see if they "fit" the observed behavior of one "representative" individual (Benito, 1976). They are not empirically tested against choice data because the test is so complicated that it is usually not worth the effort. This is because the models themselves are not *cognitively-realistic* models of the choice process. People *don't* make wholistic assignments of utility or satisfaction to each alternative and separately formulate subjective probabilities (Quinn, 1978), and then pick the alternative with the most "expected utility" (Kahneman and Tversky, 1972, 1982). Instead,

> . . . Most decisions are made in a *decomposed* fashion using *relative* comparisons. Evaluations of multidimensional alternatives are seldom wholistic in the sense of each alternative being assigned a separate level of utility. It is cognitively easier to compare alternatives on a piece-meal basis, i.e., one dimension at a time. . . . (Shoemaker, 1982)

Indeed, people do not rank order alternatives wholistically when they make a decision. They just choose one out of several alternatives without ranking them (Quinn, 1971), in which case the decision model is what Arrow (1951) calls a "choice function not built up from orderings," i.e., simply a set of rules.

A similar argument applies to the linear additive models called probit analysis and logit analysis, which have the advantage over expected utility and linear programming models of being testable with data on choices made by many rather than one individual. Unfortunately, they also are not cognitively-realistic models of the choice process. No one assigns weights to several variables and then adds them up to determine which of several outcomes is better; people compare alternatives one dimension at a time. But probit and logit analyses do have the advantage of providing a statistical test; they thus can be used alongside rule-based decision models to show whether there is a significant correlation between a particular independent variable (or decision criterion in the rule) and the decision outcome chosen. In this way, they can provide an *indirect* test of a rule-based model by showing that a particular variable is in most individuals' decision rule (Mukhopadhyay, 1984). Unfortunately, they can provide this test for only a few of the variables or criteria in an individual's decision process. Because real-life decisions can become very complicated very fast, with a great number of variables/criteria processed, as will be seen in Chapter 5, decision models should be tested *directly*.

Ethnographic decision tree modeling is thus a distinct form of decision analysis in contrast to linear additive models or even less context-sensitive, rule-based models. Because the researcher uses ethnographic eliciting techniques to specify decision criteria, he or she avoids making unrealistic behavioral assumptions and armchair propositions about how people in the real world make important decisions. Because tree models use more realistic assumptions about individuals' cognitive capabilities than do linear additive decision models, they are capable of being tested. Because they are capable of being tested against choice data from many individuals to see if they predict or not, they differ from interpretive descriptions by proposing to *test the interpretation* of an observed behavior. Ethnographic decision tree models also differ from other expert-systems or rule-based models which model the decision rules of only one expert. With the ethnographic approach, a composite or "group" model is formed from individual models of individual decision processes, and then tested against choice data from other individuals in the group. This is necessary if we want to predict the behavior of people in a group.

Tree Models Are Like Hybrids

Like modern hybrid varieties which cross varieties from different parental lines, decision tree models are models which blend quite different research approaches: on the one hand, the cyclical-discovery process of ethnographic research and, on the other, the straight-line research plan of other social sciences, e.g., economics, sociology, political science, psychology, etc. Hopefully, hybrid vigor results. The starting point is the cyclical-discovery process of ethnographic research, shown in Figure 1.1. In a circular rather than straight-line

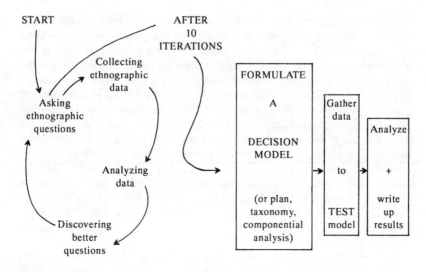

Figure 1.1 Combining the Ethnographic Research Cycle and Linear
Hypothesis-Testing Plan

fashion, the ethnographer selects a research topic, starts to ask ethnographic questions and makes field observations, makes an ethnographic
record (e.g., journal, field notes), analyzes the record and discovers
better questions to ask, and then just starts the process over again.
During the second go-round, the ethnographer asks better questions,
using "native language" categories, and gets better answers so that he
or she can formulate better questions for the third go-round (Spradley,
1980: 26-31).

After the ethnographer cycles through this discovery process for 3
to 10 iterations, he or she then goes on to the more linear, straightforward research plan of the other social sciences. In a straight-line fashion
now, he or she formulates or fully specifies the decision model to be
tested, then designs a research instrument (i.e., decides on a sampling
strategy and designs a survey, gathers the data to test the model,
analyzes the data, draws conclusions, and writes a report. Typically,
social scientists have designed and tested hypotheses or quantitative
models in this way; but newer cognitive models, e.g., decision models,
taxonomies, componential analyses, plans and scripts, can also be
formulated and tested with this plan.

Ethnographic decision tree modeling uses both of these approaches
in order to first "grasp the native's point of view, his relation to life, to
realize his vision of his world" (Malinowski, 1922) and then to model
that point of view and that vision. Use of the ethnographic-research

cycle alone is not enough; it is a necessary but not sufficient condition for good ethnographic research, which requires the researcher to follow through and test the model also during fieldwork. Combining both the ethnographic research cycle and the linear hypothesis-testing sequence takes time, of course. The ethnographic part of the process can take a few weeks or up to two years, while the model-testing part can take a few weeks or up to six months; it depends on the fieldwork situation and experience of the ethnographer (Gladwin, 1989). Generally, the decision tree modeler needs a good amount of fieldwork time, and quick and dirty research methods which claim to be rapid reconnaissance surveys (Hildebrand, 1981) will not suffice!

Decision Trees are Testable Cognitive Models

Like other models in the social sciences, decision tree models are *simplified* pictures of a part of the real world, like model trains. They are simpler than the phenomena they are supposed to explain or represent, just as a model train has some of the characteristics of a real train but not all (e.g., its size). A good model is a statement about a process and should have a sense of process in it (Lave and March, 1975: 19-49); it is evaluated in terms of its ability to correctly predict other new facts or situations or events. Thus, it has to be testable; there is no point to building a model unless one also *tests* it to see how good a representation of reality it really is.

Ethnographic decision tree modeling is therefore a formal technique used to combine individual decision makers' criteria and rules or expert systems into a computer-programmed decision model for the group which can be tested against actual choice data collected from a sample of decision makers in the group. The model is *hierarchical* rather than linear additive and takes the form of a *decision tree, table, flowchart,* or *set of if-then rules* which can be programmed in simple BASIC or FORTRAN or any number of more complicated computer languages. In Third-World country research, where light bulbs are often scarce — never mind computers — a decision tree model can even be tested with a pencil and piece of paper, as long as the researcher simulates a computer and recognizes and records an error when he or she sees one. More on this is forthcoming in Chapters 3 and 4.

A Hypothetical Example

The form of a decision tree model is thus amazingly simple, with the choice *alternatives* in a set at the top of the tree, denoted by {   } and the decision *criteria* at the nodes or diamonds of the tree denoted by <   >, and the decision *outcomes* denoted by [   ] at the ends of the *paths* of the tree. The decision maker starts at the top of the tree and, independently of other decision makers, is asked the set of questions in the criteria at the nodes of the tree, and, based on his or her responses, is "sent down" the tree on a path to a particular outcome.

The decision criteria at the nodes of the tree can be orderings of alternatives on some aspect or factor or feature of the alternatives; following Lancaster (1966) and Tversky (1972), we assume an alternative is a set of aspects (Gladwin, 1980). An example of a decision tree is given in Figure 1.2, the hypothetical model of a Third-World farmer's decision of whether to plant potatoes (the cash crop) or maize (the subsistence crop). (At this point, you should read the tree and "work through" its logic, just like you would work through a sample problem in a math text, because in order to learn how to do them, you need to practice doing them.) In this tree, criterion 1 orders the two alternatives, potatoes and maize, on the aspect profitability: "Is the profitability of potatoes > profitability of maize and beans?" The decision criteria can also be a semi-order (Luce, 1956), such that the alternatives are ordered only if one alternative is different from the other by a "just-noticeable difference δ": e.g., "Are potatoes *twice as profitable* as maize and beans?" The decision criteria can also be constraints that must be passed or satisfied on the path to a particular outcome, e.g., "Do you know how to plant potatoes?" or "Do you have the capital or credit to buy the fertilizer that potatoes need?" In either case, the criteria or constraints are discrete rather than continuous variables. The decision process is also deterministic rather than probabilistic: the alternative "potatoes" either passes the criteria or constraints with a probability of one or it does not. There are thus no probabilities—other than 0 or 1—facing the individual on each branch, as in Raiffa (1968). A decision tree is thus a sequence of discrete decision criteria, all of which have to be passed along a path to a particular outcome or choice.

In Figure 1.2, "potatoes" must pass profitability, knowledge, and capital constraints for the farmer to choose the outcome "Plant potatoes." Note that the path to this outcome can also be expressed as an if-then decision rule: "If potatoes are profitable, and you know how to plant them, and you have the capital/credit for the inputs, then plant potatoes." If the alternative "potatoes" fails any one of these criteria, the model predicts that the farmer will not plant potatoes. Here the if-then rule on one of the paths leading to the "Don't plant" outcome is "If potatoes are profitable, and you know how to plant them, but you don't have the capital/credit for the inputs, then don't plant potatoes." There are thus three paths or three rules leading to the outcome "Don't plant potatoes" because potatoes can fail either the profitability criterion or the knowledge constraint or the capital/credit constraint. Because this is the case, we say that outcomes on a tree model are not mutually-exclusive, although the paths and rules leading to the out-

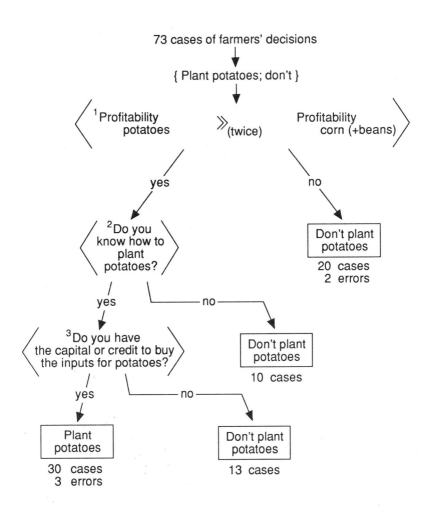

73 cases of farmers' decisions

{ Plant potatoes; don't }

[1]Profitability potatoes »(twice) Profitability corn (+beans)

yes no

[2]Do you know how to plant potatoes?

Don't plant potatoes
20 cases
2 errors

yes no

[3]Do you have the capital or credit to buy the inputs for potatoes?

Don't plant potatoes
10 cases

yes no

Plant potatoes
30 cases
3 errors

Don't plant potatoes
13 cases

Figure 1.2 A Hypothetical Example of a Cropping Decision Model

comes are different. Note that each path of the tree corresponds to one if-then decision rule, and *the tree as a whole is equivalent to a set of decision rules or a decision table with the same set of rules* (Gladwin, 1975; Young, 1980: 116).

Once the decision model is "built" or programmed, based on interviews with one set of decision makers, it can be tested for accuracy in predicting choices made by another sample of decision makers from the same group. In Figure 1.2, the model makes an *error* if it predicts that the farmer plants potatoes but he or she does not or if it predicts that the farmer does not plant potatoes but he or she does. In the simplest test of the model, errors are counted on each path, and a simple "success rate" for the model is calculated by dividing the total number of successes by the total number of cases on all paths.

If the decision model successfully predicts 85 to 90% of the individual choices of the individuals in the group, it is assumed to be an adequate model of the individual decision process for that group of individuals. If not, it's back to the drawing board for the researcher, who may try to recombine or "juggle" the decision criteria or paths of the tree in another order or even do more ethnographic fieldwork and find previously-omitted decision criteria. Failures of decision tree models to predict well may be due to any number of reasons: e.g., the researcher has gotten the combination of criteria wrong, ignored or misspecified some important criteria, or even ignored some of the real-life alternatives open to the decision makers. (We return to these errors in modeling in Chapter 4.)

In real-life decisions, of course, the world is much more complicated than the simple hypothetical decision tree in Figure 1.2 suggests, and a model of a real-world decision process starts off simple, but, after the model-building process, usually ends up quite complex. Such was the case of the cropping-decision model formulated to explain to government policy planners why Indian farmers in the Guatemalan Highlands always plant maize, the subsistence crop, whereas government planners want farmers to grow and sell higher-valued cash crops and buy maize in the marketplace. That particular model — a two-stage, four-figure model with a 90% success rate — was built during interviews with 60 farmers in six agroclimatic zones and tested with decision data from another 118 farmers in the Highlands. The model tells politicians who conclude that "maize is not the right crop for the Highlands" that subsistence maize has primary importance to farmers, that it will be planted first, before the usual cash crops, and that the profitability of every cash crop is first compared to that of maize before another cash crop. Given this conclusion of the model, a policy recommendation can be made to government planners, namely to concentrate on agronomic research designed to increase maize yields so that more cash crops can be planted *after* maize is planted. This should prove to be the *most effective crop-diversification strategy* in the Highlands, capable of reaching the majority of the farmers. Because this model has been published in several places (Gladwin, 1980, 1982a, 1983, 1989), the reader is referred to those papers for more detail.

A Real-Life Decision Example: Credit for Fertilizer in Malawi

Instead, as an example of a real-life choice of applied importance, let's use the African farmer's decision to get credit for modern inputs, namely fertilizer.[1] This decision is a crucial one for African government planners facing a "food crisis" in their cities and trying to increase the food surplus produced by small farmers in the countryside, because credit use is correlated with fertilizer use, which is linked to food surpluses. (And, for our purposes here, it will illustrate points made in later chapters about how to model and how not to model.)

The decision is important because seasonal credit now reaches only *16%* out of the 1.3 million farmers in Malawi, or 206,000 farmers. Only about *6%* of land owned by smallholders is currently financed by credit, mainly through "farmers' clubs," whose membership is limited to male household heads and single women household heads who do not have a male to get fertilizer for them. Default rates have been a low 3% of the loans. But there are also women's clubs in Malawi which give credit to both married and single women, through the government's Women's Programme, for groundnut seed and/or fertilizer; their default rate is even lower than that of the farmers' clubs. In 1985/86, credit volume was 19.96 million "kwachas" at interest rates of 10 percent. Yet, the expansion of these clubs has been slow. For example, in 1982/83 there were 6,654 farmers' clubs in Malawi with 156,703 members, and four years later, there were 8,045 clubs with 206,409 members to equal an expansion of 17.3% between 1982 and 1986.

Because less than one-fifth of Malawi's farmers are now members of credit groups, one has to ask who are the favored members of the groups and who are excluded and *why.* Although previous studies have shown that 69% of Malawi's full-time farmers are women (Kydd and Christiansen, 1982), that women provide 50% of the farm labor (Dixon, 1982), and that 28% of households in Malawi are headed by women, women household heads in 1986/87 account for only 25% of credit club members. It is not clear whether they are excluded from credit clubs because they are women or because most (72%) of them are small farmers with less than one hectare of land.

To answer these questions, smallholders' decisions to join a credit club were modeled and decision criteria elicited during personal interviews with nine farmers in Lilongwe and Kasungu districts.[2] The model is in Figures 1.3 and 1.4, with the alternatives the farmer must choose between listed in the parentheses at the top of the tree, e.g., {Get credit for some fertilizer via a farmers' or women's club; don't get credit at all}. The model was further tested in interviews with 30 additional farmers in Lilongwe, Kasungu, and Salima districts; but more on this in Chapter 3. The tree model in Figures 1.3 and 1.4 thus combines in a logical order the reasons why some farmers *get credit for fertilizer*

18

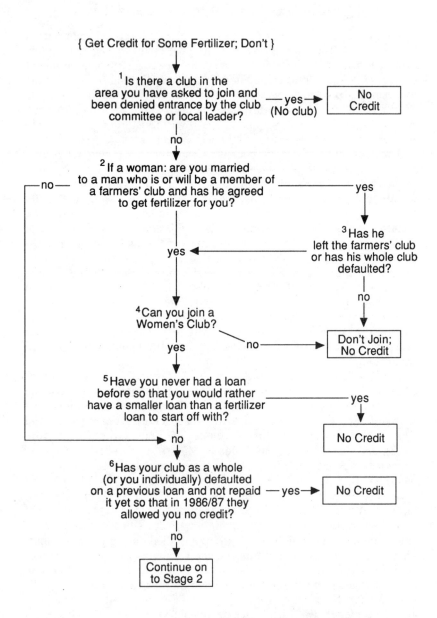

Figure 1.3 Stage 1 of the Malawi Farmer's Decision to Get Credit for Some
Fertilizer Via a Farmers' of Women's Club

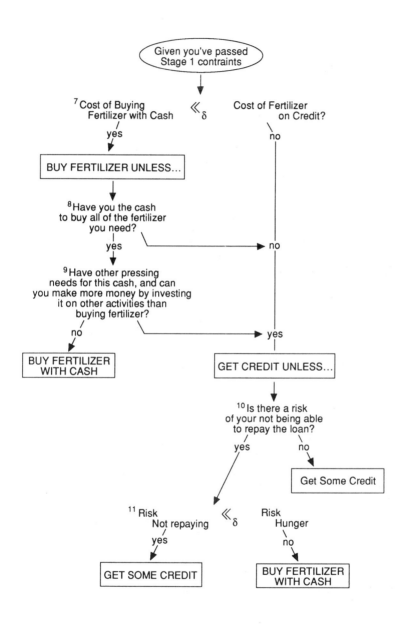

Figure 1.4 Stage 2 of the Malawi Farmer's Credit Decision

ELIMINATION BY ASPECTS *ORDERING ASPECTS*

while others decide to *buy it* with cash from ADMARC, the state marketing board and sole distributor.

The first six criteria in the tree in Figure 1.3 are criteria that eliminate a farmer from a credit club; this first stage of the decision process happens rapidly, often subconsciously or *preattentively* in routine decisions (Gladwin and Murtaugh, 1980) and is thus called "elimination-by-aspects" (Tversky, 1972; Gladwin, 1980). For example, some farmers are rejected for admission to a farmers' club by other club members because they are too poor, have too small a farm or "garden," or live in the wrong village (criterion 1). In these cases, not being in a club is *a given* for them, and they will not spend more time deciding whether or not to get credit; they know that the credit option has been eliminated for them. Other stage-one preattentive criteria in this decision include: the (woman) farmer is married to a member of a farmers' club and he by law must get the fertilizer on credit *for* her (criterion 2), unless he (or his whole club) has defaulted on a previous loan and now cannot receive credit (criterion 3); there is no women's club in the area which gives credit for fertilizer directly to the women (criterion 4); women lack confidence in or familiarity with credit clubs so that they won't take the risk of a big fertilizer loan (criterion 5); the farmer or the whole club cannot now receive credit due to a previous default on their part (criterion 6). If any of these conditions holds, credit as an option is eliminated for the farmer whose data are "put down" the tree.

If the farmer "passes" these constraints successfully, he or she passes to the *ordering aspect* in criterion 7, on which he or she minimizes the cost of acquiring fertilizer. This ordering aspect signals the beginning of stage two in the model, the conscious or hard-core part of the decision process. (The ordering aspect is similar to micro-economists' choice principle of "maximization subject to constraints"; but more on this in Chapters 4 and 5.) If the cost of buying fertilizer is much less than the cost of getting it on credit, the farmer "goes down" the left hand branch of the tree and *"Buys fertilizer unless . . ."* other constraints get in the way which lead him or her back to the *"Get credit unless . . ."* (right-hand) branch of the tree. These "unless conditions" include a lack of cash to buy all the fertilizer needed (criterion 8), or enough cash to buy fertilizer but not other needs for the cash such as school fees, clothing, etc. (criterion 9). These criteria will send the farmer to the right hand or "Get credit" branch of the tree. If the farmer has other uses for the cash and so needs the credit, but thinks there's a risk of not being able to repay the loan (criterion 10), *and* this risk of non-repayment is *greater* than the risk of "inviting hunger" if maize varieties are grown without fertilizer (criterion 11), then he or she should buy the fertilizer with cash. Why is not repaying a credit loan so risky? Farmers in default report that other club members and extension agents steal their animals, oxcarts, and even the doors and roofs to their houses to hold until the farmer or a family member repays the loan. All the assets that the farmer has accumulated can be wiped out if the farmer can't repay the fertilizer loan in a bad year: hence, non-repayment can be very risky indeed. Some farmers, in contrast, "go down" the right-hand branch of the tree and *get the credit* for at least some of the needed fertilizer if they think there is little difference in the costs of acquiring fertilizer on credit versus with cash, *or* they do not have all the cash needed to buy it, *or* they have other more pressing needs for this cash *and* can also pass the risk constraints. The farmer will take the risks of credit, i.e., of not being able to repay the loan, if he or she thinks "You invite hunger if you grow local maize without fertilizer" because the yields will be too low, and he or she judges the danger of hunger to be greater than the danger of not being able to repay the fertilizer loan (criterion 11).

Let's Get Going

How can we tell if this model is any good? How can you build similar decision models and draw policy conclusions? In Chapter 2 we begin with the simplest kind of decision to model: the "Do it; don't do it" decision. We also begin to do homework problems in Chapter 2 because decision tree modeling is *learning by doing*. In Chapter 3, we test this simple model (and the credit-decision model), revise it, and compare it to the revised model, based on that test. Chapter 4 then warns the reader how *not* to do it and how to recognize common errors in model building. We discuss more complicated, multi-stage and multi-alternative models and series of sequential models in Chapter 5. We talk about how to cope with decision models that suddenly start to expand — like *The Thing,* the being in the movie of the same name that clones itself at subzero temperatures and becomes more and more huge and complicated — from one tree to five or six, as we elicit unless conditions to the original unless conditions and exceptions to the exceptions to the rule (Harris, 1974). Chapter 6 concludes by answering the question "So what?" Of what use are decision tree models to the applied social scientist?

2. HOW TO MODEL SIMPLE "DO IT; DON'T DO IT" DECISIONS

This chapter describes how to get started modeling decisions and how to use simple elicitation procedures and contrast questions. It explains how to choose the sample of decision makers to interview and how to build a composite decision model from many individuals' decision rules. Summarized are rules of interviewing, use of contrast questions, and use of quantitative data to set up a contrast question. If a contrast isn't available in one informant's data, the researcher can contrast different choice behaviors of different informants. Also explained is how to turn an ad hoc composite model into a more logical one. The chapter starts the reader modeling the decision to go to a fast-food restaurant near the university for lunch and ends with a fairly comprehensive example of how to build a decision model, using the college freshman's decision to buy a breakfast contract.

Given the treelike or rule-based form of decision model described in Chapter 1, you, the researcher, must get started building the model. How? Because you're new at this business, you can think of the process of model building as one of following a cognitive plan which has steps in it which tell you what to do to build decision models. Like most cognitive plans, it also has some decision points embedded in it. Later, this plan will become so routine that we can think of it as a script, like the script in a play that tells the actor what to do or say (Schank and Abelson, 1977). But now, because you are new at this, realize that you have to follow the plan carefully to model your informants' decision processes. The steps in the plan are the following.

STEP 1.

Decide which decision you're studying. Suppose you're a professor or student at the university and you want to study a simple, ordinary, routine decision like the decision to go to a restaurant. You've got a lot of work to do and want to do this modeling fast. Should you just go out and elicit decision criteria from people at your favorite restaurant? No. In order to specify the decision criteria correctly, you first have to be clear about just what decision you are studying. Unfortunately, there are any number of decisions involved in the seemingly innocent restaurant decision. Which of these decisions are you going to study?

- *whether* or not to go to a restaurant in general versus brown-bagging it in your office versus going home for lunch
- which restaurant in town to go to for lunch
- which restaurant in town to go to for breakfast
- which restaurant in town to go to for dinner
- whether or not to go off campus or on campus
- whether or not to go to a fast-food; take-out; or classy, sit-down, take-your-time restaurant for lunch
- which fast-food restaurant in town to go to for lunch

- which fast-food restaurant near the university to go to for lunch
- whether or not to go to McDonald's near the university for lunch

Clearly, there are a lot of decisions involved in going to a restaurant, and, although some of the decision criteria may be the same in all these models, some of them may be different. *A priori,* you can't assume they are the same. (A good ethnographer tries to minimize his or her own ethnocentricity by not making assumptions.) In addition, you have to decide: are you studying one of these decisions or more than one? (If the decisions are interrelated and recursive, you may start off with a simple decision model but end up with a multi-stage or time-sequential decision model, to be discussed in Chapter 5.)

Let's assume you opt to study one decision, and it's simple: the decision of which fast-food restaurant near the university to go to for lunch. Note that this is more complicated than the simplest kind of "Do it; don't do it" decision: whether or not to go to McDonald's near the university for lunch. But you also need a challenge in your life right now and opt for a more exciting decision to study. Now can you elicit decision criteria? Not yet.

STEP 2.

Decide on the set of alternatives in the decision. Another complication is that there may be more than one set of *alternatives,* and each brings its own set of constraints with it because real-life decisions are not made in a controlled laboratory experiment but are made *in context,* where the context is historical, material, social, and environmental. In the restaurant decision, for example, the set of alternatives can be:

- {brown bag it; go out to a restaurant; go home}
- {set of all restaurants in town}
- {set of all restaurants in town that serve lunch}
- {set of all McDonald's restaurants in town}
- {set of all restaurants near the university that serve lunch, on and off campus}
- {set of all take-outs within walking distance of your office}
- {set of all fast-food restaurants near the university}
- {McDonald's, Burger King, Kentucky Fried Chicken near campus, none of these}
- {set of all McDonald's restaurants near the university}
- {Go to McDonald's on 13th St.; don't}.

Of course, once you decide on the decision you're studying in step 1, some of these sets are eliminated. But even if you've narrowed the study down to the decision of whether or not to go to a fast-food place near the university for lunch, you still have to decide between these sets of alternatives:

- {set of all fast-food restaurants near the University}
- {McDonald's, Burger King, Kentucky Fried Chicken near campus, none of these}
- {set of all McDonald's restaurants near the university}
- {Go to McDonald's on 13th St.; don't}
- {Go to Burger King on University Ave.; don't}
- {Go to Kentucky Fried Chicken on 12th Ave.; don't}.

Which one do you choose? At this point, you're ready to give up on the whole decision modeling idea, so you opt for the simplest set of alternatives to study because this is all new to you:

- {Go to McDonald's on 13th St.; don't}.

Now can you elicit decision criteria? Well, no.

STEP 3.

Remember how to conduct an ethnographic interview (Spradley 1979: 61-66); *find an informant in your cultural scene and practice on him or her.* In this first interview, don't worry about eliciting decision criteria; don't start off with "And how do you decide whether to go to McDonald's or Burger King?" Just follow Spradley's rules for interviewing in order to learn about the cultural scene, in this case the set of fast-food restaurants near the university open at lunchtime. To see how you're doing as an ethnographer, tape yourself, transcribe the tape, and analyze your performance, just as Spradley did.

Remember that Spradley emphasized the similarities between an informal conversation and an ethnographic interview, as opposed to your running through a carefully planned out, preordained set of questions which the informant doesn't dare to interrupt. You should start with friendly greetings ("Hiya, how are you?") and explain your project to informants to put them at ease; you should tell them how interested you are in knowing what they know. Then you should follow up with a "grand tour" description question ("Tell me about it") to get the informant talking. If the informant is reluctant, you should again explain that you don't really know anything about this cultural scene — and the informant is an expert. In fact, throughout the interview, you should express cultural ignorance. You could play Colombo, who's not too bright but always gets the killer, to convince informants that *they're the experts* and you're the student sitting at their feet. Or you could wear funny, squeaky shoes like Hercule Poirot, whom nobody takes seriously; or you could act like a sweet, innocent, but nosy old lady like Miss Marple, who threatens nobody by her presence. All these famous detectives express cultural ignorance. They don't assume they know what the informant knows; to avoid their own ethnocentrism, they check on whether they share knowledge with the informant.

Once informants open up, you can incorporate their native expressions (e.g., jargon like "quarter pounders with cheese") in your next question, or you try a "mini-tour" descriptive question (e.g., "What do you do to order lunch in this place?"), or you can elicit a plan (e.g., "Could you start at the beginning of lunch, a typical lunch at McDonald's, and tell me what goes on?"). When there's a pause in the conversation, and with eye-to-eye contact, you should again express interest in what the informant is saying. Don't be looking at your notes or preparing your next question when the informant is talking; *listen* to what the informant is saying. "Follow through" from his or her responses, i.e., make up your next question after you have understood his or her previous response. *Respond* to the informant during the interview.

During the interview, you should *never ask a leading question,* i.e., a question with the answer in it: e.g., "Do you not go out with the waitresses here because you think they're dogs?" or "Do you not order Big Mac's because you don't have the money?" or "Why don't you like quarter pounders with cheese? Do you think they have too many calories?" In these cases of leading questions, the ethnographer is so anxious to get information out of the informant that he or she is losing the information because, when pressed, most informants will agree with the leading question, and then the chance to get valid information is lost. Informants will rarely contradict a leading question; and, unfortunately, the question sounds stupid when rephrased a second time so that it's properly open-ended. For the same reason, you should never correct informants or subtly try to get them to change their minds. You may, however, ask a *verification* question in which you restate what the informant just said and then ask if you've got it right.

Your aim is to get the informant to correct *your* mistaken ethnocentric ideas about his or her cultural scene, and people won't contradict you unless they feel comfortable doing it. So, you should never make the informant feel dumb. Make him or her feel *macho/macha!* This is not always easy when there is a difference in class, education, and/or wealth between yourself and poor informants in Third World countries or United States inner cities. You are a possible "patron" in the eyes of the informants, and your pretending to be an ignorant outsider may seem phoney to people who've learned to survive by forming patron/client relationships with richer, more powerful people. One solution is to repeatedly explain that, while you may be a professor or student at the university, you are not an expert in the informant's culture, whereas he or she is. Another solution is to act dumb, as Columbo does, or laid-back and almost timid, as the anthropologist Charles Frake (the real master) does.

In order to build rapport, some researchers don't go into a model-building interview with a formal questionnaire typed out (Hildebrand, 1981) because questionnaires don't inspire informants to start talking. Instead, they make up a checklist of information needed on a note-card, stick it in their pockets, and pull it out to check it over during the interview. They then stick it back in their pockets and resume eye-to-eye contact while asking questions. Personally, I don't usually follow this practice after the first few interviews. While I agree that rapport is more easily built without a questionnaire, I don't remember all the questions I should ask during the interview, plus I tend to forget some of the informant's responses. In step 7, therefore, I present two methods of building a "composite" decision model, with and without a formal questionnaire.

At the end of your interview, you should say "Thanks," take your leave, and—elicit decision criteria? No, not yet.

STEP 4.

In addition to ethnographic interviews, do some participation observation (Spradley, 1980). If you are studying farmers' fertilizer decisions (e.g., to fertilize plants more often), make an appointment to observe them doing the fertilizing (Gladwin, 1979a); or help them do the first weeding. Observe more than one informant, and try to observe contrasting choice behavior. Granted, this is easier to do when the decision is how often the informant fertilizes and harder when the decision is how often the informant takes drugs!

To study the latter decision legally, you have to rely on eliciting techniques. In general, asking decision makers about how they make *their* decisions, instead of mutely standing by watching, seems the natural starting point in the modeling process. But remember Miss Marple's advice in the *Sleeping Murder:* don't be gullible. Always check out with another source the information that an informant gives you. The best way to check on what people tell you is to watch their behavior and see if their actions match their words. If you observe a contrast in what they say versus what they do, go back and ask them to explain the contrast; this will help elicit decision criteria in step 6.

STEP 5.

Decide on the sample of decision makers to use to build the model.
Decide when and where to interview them. As in most scientific studies, you can't just interview your friends or anyone who's ever made the decision you're studying. Instead, you should select a sample that's as *representative* as possible of the population of people who make the decision, in this case, people who go — and don't go — to McDonald's for lunch. Unlike other studies which use *one* sample to gather quantitative data representative of the population, to build your decision model you should interview *two* subsets of people, those who go and those who don't go, to capture as much variation as possible in your sample. You need two samples to elicit the reasons for going to the restaurant from those who, in fact, went to McDonald's; and you need to elicit the constraints which prevent some people from going from people who did not go to McDonald's today. Why? It is impossible to elicit from the doers and the goers some of the constraints which prevent other people from doing or going because they've overcome these constraints and have forgotten them. It is easy, however, to elicit these constraints from those who don't do X or do go to Y now, today, at this time t. Note that you want people who make this decision now, at this time t, not five years ago; because psychological studies show memory is extremely short-term.

For the simplest decision to go or not to go to McDonald's for lunch now, at time t, the model-building sample should be one subset of (10 to 20) people now eating lunch at McDonald's and willing to talk to you over lunch and one subset of (10 to 20) people not now eating lunch at McDonald's. The latter set of people can be outside McDonald's innocently walking down the street, or eating at Burger King, or sitting on the university lawn eating their lunch, or trying to work in their offices, or whatever. Here again, your aim is to get a representative sample of the population, and if you can get a random sample, go for it. Otherwise, use stratified sampling, and include as much variation in your sample as you can: young and old, men and women, rich and poor, Whites and Blacks, Hispanics, Asians, etc.

How many informants should be interviewed in the model-building stage? Here, my motto is: "Produce results, not perfection!" At this stage in previous studies, I have interviewed 20 to 30 informants in a relatively homogeneous culture, such as one village, because the central-limit theorem assures us that all distributions tend to the normal when n approaches 25 (Gladwin, 1976). When doing a regional study of more than one village (or one cultural scene), however, I have interviewed 90 to 120 informants at this stage and an equal number again in the testing stage (Gladwin, 1982a). Frankly, I don't know if these samples are big enough; the question of "How many is enough" is a complex one, and really deserves further study by a statistician. In the meantime, let's proceed to elicit decision criteria.

STEP 6.

Select (i.e., specify) the decision criteria or constraints to use in the model. You should decide which information is actually considered by decision makers when they make a particular decision as opposed to information that, while interesting and important, is unused as decision criteria in this particular decision. Quinn (1978), for example, points out that the rank-ordering of alternatives is interesting information for the ethnographer to have; but when making decisions, informants don't seem to do it, except on a specific ordering aspect. (We'll return to the "ordering aspect" in Chapters 4 and 5.) This is the hardest part of the job of modeling: the sifting and sorting of all the information informants give you in order to identify the "real" decision criteria that "cut" the sample into the two subsets mentioned above: those who do X (e.g., go to McDonald's today for lunch) and those who don't.

Because the modeler is looking for key phrases or linguistic "frames" to represent decision criteria, it is best to tape-record every interview, whether or not it is in one's native language. Immediately following each interview, the ethnographer should briefly describe the informant and record on tape any interpretations of the decision context that he or she might have, e.g., the unmentioned presence of the informant's gang of twenty friends also eating lunch at McDonald's. Even though the whole tape might not be transcribed, it should be listened to later while the modeler is penciling out the decision model and ordering decision criteria in steps 6c and 7 below.

Discovering Decision Criteria

There are several ways to elicit decision criteria, both direct and indirect, but they all require the interviewer to look for *contrasts* in decision behavior, ask an informant to explain any contrasts, and then test that explanation on another informant. This process is repeated until the criteria are specified correctly, i.e., until most of the informants' decision behavior is explained by the criteria.

The steps include:

STEP 6a.

Look for contrasts over decision makers, over space or locations (with one decision maker), or over time (with one decision maker). Examples of contrasts include freshmen college students who do and who don't buy a breakfast contract to eat breakfast in the college cafeteria. Here, the students themselves provide the contrast, and the ethnographer asks each one why he or she does or does not get a breakfast contract. Another example is provided by a Puebla farmer who, in the same year, fertilizes his maize and beans at planting time only on his irrigated fields, but not on his rain-fed fields. A contrast over time is provided by a person who this week eats lunch at McDonald's on Wednesday but not on Thursday.

STEP 6b. *CONTRAST QUESTIONS*

Once a contrast in decision behavior is found, the interviewer elicits the criterion by asking, "Why did person$_1$ do X but person$_2$ do Y?" or "Why did you do this in space X but that in space Y?" or "Why did you do this at time$_1$ but that at time$_2$?" In the decision of whether or not to buy a breakfast contract at the college cafeteria, the interviewer simply asks students directly, "Why did you buy the breakfast contract? Why didn't your roommate buy the breakfast contract?" In the Puebla farmer's fertilizer decision, the farmer is asked, "Why did you fertilize at planting in this field but not in that field?" In the restaurant decision, the person eating lunch at McDonald's today is asked, "Did you also eat lunch yesterday at McDonald's? Why not?"

Spradley (1979: Chapter 5) lists fancier ways to ask contrast questions. They include first eliciting a taxonomy of native terms used by informants (e.g., the names of games played at recess by second graders) and then asking direct contrast questions ("Why is 'making fun of others' termed 'goofing around' and not 'a trick'?"). They also include sorting tasks ("Would you sort these cards into two or more piles in terms of some way the cards are alike and different? Put them in different piles this time") and the triads test ("Which two of these are alike and which one is different?"). These techniques can apply to different decision behavior as well as different native terms.

One more piece of advice in using contrast questions and eliciting decision criteria is seen in the cartoon "Conrad" reprinted with permission from Bill Schorr. The decision context is that the princess, who needs advice about her love life, is having tea with her fairy godmother. The fairy godmother's final piece of advice, "Let's think of some obvious decision criteria Conrad could be using before assuming the esoteric," is good advice for us as well as for the princess. People do use obvious decision criteria, maybe because they have so many decisions to make all day long that they *must* simplify them to conserve their mental energies (Quinn, 1971; Tversky and Kahneman, 1981). Look, for example, at how many decisions you've already made, and you haven't even built your first decision tree. One way to simplify is to use common sense when formulating decision criteria. Implications: the

ethnographer who, like the princess, prefers complicated, esoteric explanations is going to miss the boat on prediction rates!

STEP 6c.

After the decision criteria are elicited from one decision maker, you have your first decision tree. So, it's time to sit down in a quiet place, take out paper and pencil, review what your first informant said, and draw the tree. You might think this is premature after your first twenty-minute interview. However, it will clarify your thinking and make the second and third interviews easier and help you get more information out of them. Let's see how another neophyte at decision modeling did it.

Example: The Freshman's Decision to Buy a Breakfast Contract[3]

For incoming freshmen at most colleges, an immediate decision one has to make is whether or not to purchase a breakfast contract to eat breakfast in the college cafeteria. The breakfast contract is purchased separately from other meals and often before the freshman ever arrives on campus. The decision makers in this study lived in an all-women's dorm with a cafeteria in the basement; they were interviewed by another freshman, Karen Rain. The set of alternatives are either to buy the breakfast contract or not to buy it (and presumably eat nothing or eat in one's room). Serving hours for breakfast are 7:15 A.M. until 9:00 A.M. on weekdays and 8:00 A.M. until 9:00 A.M. on Saturdays. Meals are varied, and students are free to eat as much as they want and to come back for seconds. The one restriction is that no food is to be taken out of the cafeteria.

In order to build the decision model, 10 freshmen girls were interviewed. The first interview was with Lucy Rhee, a College of Arts and Sciences biology major from Ohio, who said that she chose *not* to buy a breakfast contract because she had not been eating breakfast since the fifth grade. She prefers to sleep as late as possible in the morning, and she felt that missing a paid breakfast on a regular basis would be a waste of money. Her decision is represented by the tree in Figure 2.1a.

Question$_1$: What decision rule is Lucy following?

Answer: If you're not used to eating breakfast at home, and you want to sleep as late as possible in the morning, and you feel the contract is a waste of money if you don't eat every day, then don't buy the contract. Note that each decision criterion becomes an *if*-condition in the decision rule, and the decision outcome follows the word *then*.

Homework 2.1: Develop a tree model of your first informant's decision of whether or not to eat lunch at McDonald's today, trying to avoid the following common problem experienced by other uninitiated tree modelers.

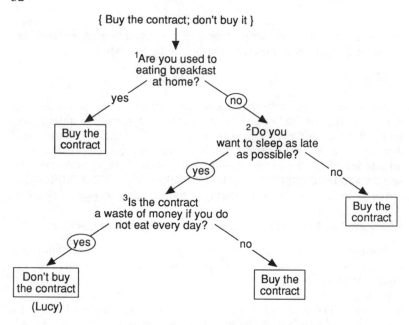

Figure 2.1a Lucy's Decision Not to Buy a Breakfast Contract

Common Problem 1: At this point, you can make your first mistake and build a model which is just *too simple* to be a good model of a real-life decision process. Suppose, in the breakfast contract decision, you listened to Lucy's explanation of why she didn't buy the breakfast contract and recognized only the first criterion, "Are you used to eating breakfast at home?" as a valid decision criterion. Let's assume that you put this criterion in the model of Figure 2.1b. What's wrong with this model? If you now go on to the second informant and elicit only one decision criterion from her, and likewise with all 10 informants, you'll end up with a too-simple, pure "elimination-by-aspects" model of the decision process, seen in Figure 4.1 and discussed in more depth in Chapter 4. This too-simple model looks like a checklist and may predict decisions from your first ten informants because most of the predictions are made by the first criterion. However, it won't predict decisions of a broader sample of decision makers because you haven't captured the internal logic of the process or the "emic" reasoning of the decision makers. The way to avoid this problem now is to *probe further* when the informant gives you only one simple decision criterion. Ask her, "Well, how does that affect whether or not you get the breakfast contract?" You would then elicit criteria 2 and 3, as Karen Rain did, and figure out how these three criteria fit together in the logical framework of the tree in Figure 2.1a. After the first informant's tree is formulated,

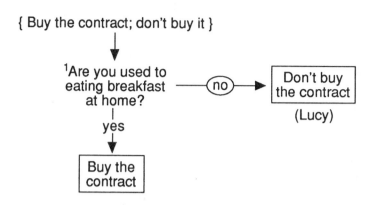

Figure 2.1b Lucy's Decision Not to Buy a Breakfast Contract

it's time to go on to the next informant and see if these informants share any decision criteria in step 7.

STEP 7.

Build a composite decision model for the group from the individual decision trees. There are two methods at this crucial step: an *indirect* method, whereby you build one "composite" decision model for the group as you go along interviewing the first sample of informants, and a more *direct* method, whereby you build an individual model of each informant's decision process (i.e., ten little models) and put them together later into one composite decision model.

The Indirect Method

After the decision criteria are elicited from one decision maker, the interviewer goes on to another decision maker and tests them on him or her. If they work perfectly, the criteria are "correctly specified." This occurs if they *cut* the sample of (by this time, two) decision makers into two subsets: those who pass or satisfy the criteria and decide to do X and those who fail the criteria and decide not to do X. If the criteria are not correctly specified, i.e., they do not cut, the interviewer must acquire more information about the cultural context, add new criteria, revise some of the old criteria or the order of the criteria, and retest the new version on more informants. What new information might this be? In the case of the fast-food restaurant decision, it might be a taxonomy of all fast-food restaurants near the university, or meal plans of university students, or dieting goals of men versus women students, etc. All this information might affect the decision, and be part of the context within which the decision is made, thereby generating decision criteria which should be in the model. After new criteria are added and/or some criteria are revised, the testing process is repeated until the criteria cut, i.e., predict decision behavior.

In the first example of the decision to buy a breakfast contract, using this method requires the interviewer to write down the decision criteria in the form of questions and ask the second informant:

(1) Did you buy the breakfast contract?   Yes_____ No_____

(2) Are you used to eating breakfast at home? Yes_____ No_____

(3) Do you want to sleep as late as possible in the
  morning?   Yes_____ No_____

(4) Do you think the contract is a waste of money if
  you do not eat breakfast every day? Yes_____ No_____

Note that in question 1 we ask the second informant what her decision behavior is *before* we ask her the questions representing the decision criteria. This is because we do not want our questioning procedure in itself to push the informant into telling us she gets the breakfast contract when in fact, she doesn't. (Again, this is all too possible when there is a class or wealth or status difference between the informant and the interviewer. In order to please the interviewer, the poor informant may claim to do things not actually done, e.g., the adoption of the newest agricultural technologies.)

If this set of four questions predicts exactly what the second informant does, we have our decision criteria perfectly specified — so far. In fact, this is what happened in the example of the breakfast contract decision. The second informant was Nancy Fisher, also a College of Arts and Sciences biology major from New York, who does have a breakfast contract. Nancy said she decided to get the contract because she has always had three meals a day and is used to eating breakfast in the morning (question 1). She added that she has early classes every day and so does not mind getting up to eat breakfast when it is served. Nancy's decision criteria can be put in the tree in Figure 2.2.

However, the opposite happened when Karen interviewed the next informant, Melissa Meltzer, who does not have a breakfast contract. The journalism major from New Jersey stated that she wasn't used to eating breakfast at home and she likes to sleep late. But when asked question 4 above, she claimed it wasn't so much a question of the contract's being a waste of money — because, after all, it was her parents' money, and they had lots of it, but that she and her roommate had bought a small

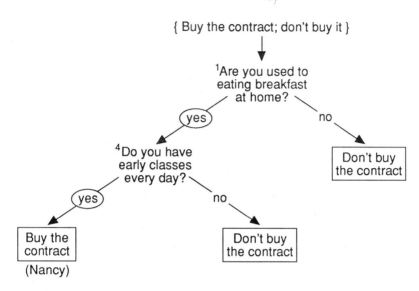

Figure 2.2 Nancy's Decision to Buy a Contract

refrigerator and breakfast foods to keep in their room so that they could have breakfast on the occasions when they were hungry in the morning. Her decision tree is seen in Figure 2.3. Clearly, the decision criteria which worked for the first two informants did not work for the third, and Karen, the interviewer, had to add a new criterion and question 5 to her questionnaire:

(5) Do you have food and a refrigerator in your room
    in case you're hungry?   Yes_____ No_____

A similar problem developed with the next informant, Tracy Taub, an applied voice major in the School of Music from Florida. Tracy said that she did not buy a breakfast contract because she does not eat breakfast at home usually, but when asked question 3 above, she said no, she does not sleep as late as possible in the morning. (And the model fails.) When asked to explain why she didn't buy a breakfast contract, Tracy said she did not consider sleeping late as a factor in deciding not to buy the contract because she could easily eat breakfast in the time that she has every morning. She just is not hungry in the morning. Again, the decision criteria that predicted the first two informants' decisions did not predict Tracy's decision, and her decision tree is shown in Figure 2.4. Karen then added another criteria and question (6) to her questionnaire:

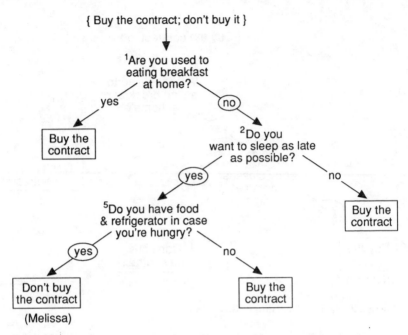

Figure 2.3 Melissa's Decision Not to Buy a Contract

(6) Are you usually hungry in the morning?   Yes_____ No_____

Similar problems occurred with the next two informants. Liz Olson, a College of Arts and Sciences student from Minnesota, did not buy a contract (Figure 2.5) because she does not usually eat breakfast, and she likes to sleep late. She also said that her brother, who is a college senior, advised her not to buy the breakfast contract because he had never used it. Carol Want, however, does have a breakfast contract (Figure 2.6). She is a chemical engineering major in the Technological Institute from Indiana. While she wasn't especially brought up on big breakfasts and isn't that hungry in the morning, she bought the contract because she needs three good meals a day, and she is up early every morning for grinding-hard math and science classes.

Homework 2.2: Figure out what questions Karen should add to her questionnaire now, to check on Liz's and Carol's new decision criteria with other informants.

The Direct Method

Alternatively, the interviewer may opt to be more direct with each informant and just ask why he or she does what he or she does, and elicit

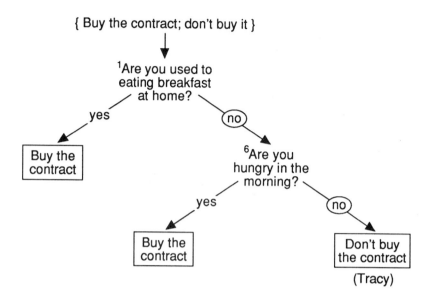

Figure 2.4 Tracy's Decision Not to Buy a Contract

his or her criteria, and draw his or her decision tree, and see if the second tree is the same as the tree of the first informant. If the trees are the same, which is unlikely, there's no problem. If they are different, then the interviewer has two different decision trees which have to be combined into a group or composite tree model in step 8.

Homework 2.3: Build an individual decision tree for each of the remaining four informants Karen Rain interviewed in her model-building sample, based on the following profiles of their decisions.

Sony Martinez does not have a breakfast contract because she is used to eating only two meals a day and sleeping as late as possible in the morning. One of her older brothers also advised her against buying a contract because she would not need it if she continued her present habits.

Karen Goldschmidt decided against buying a breakfast contract because she likes to sleep late in the morning and is not used to eating breakfast at home. She felt that missing breakfast because of oversleeping would be a waste of the money spent on the contract.

Marilyn Poyner did not buy a contract because she felt that it is just as easy for her to make her own breakfast in her room every morning. She is used to eating breakfast, but, since her classes are not always early in the morning, she knew that she would miss breakfast on

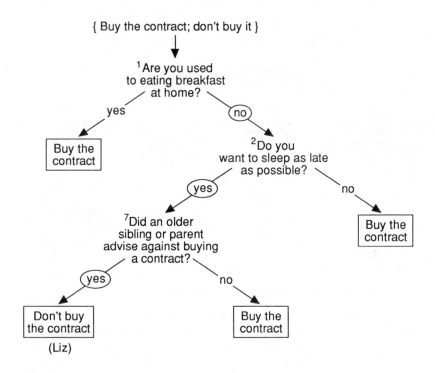

{ Buy the contract; don't buy it }

[1]Are you used to eating breakfast at home?

yes → Buy the contract

no → [2]Do you want to sleep as late as possible?

yes → [7]Did an older sibling or parent advise against buying a contract?

no → Buy the contract

yes → Don't buy the contract (Liz)

no → Buy the contract

Figure 2.5 Liz's Decision Not to Buy a Contract

a regular basis. Marilyn does have a refrigerator and breakfast food in her room.

Carrie Pidrak did not buy a breakfast contract because she does not usually eat breakfast, and she likes to sleep late. The Liberal Arts major from Illinois said that she has a refrigerator and breakfast foods in her room if she should want breakfast.

By now, the reader should see the advantage of the direct method of decision modeling, namely that it eliminates an inevitably stilted, boring, and unnatural questionnaire and so allows a more natural ethnographic interview of each informant. It has the disadvantage, however, that the interviewer doesn't ask the same questions to each informant in the model-building sample and so doesn't check out each criterion to see whether other informants also consider it a valid decision criterion, as is done with the indirect method. But both methods work, and it's time to move on to step 8. If you've done your homework, you now

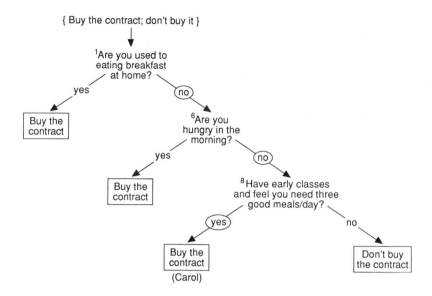

Figure 2.6 Carol's Decision to Buy a Contract

have ten different decision trees from ten informants;[4] it's time to combine them in a logical fashion.

STEP 8.

Combine all the different decision trees from all informants in the model-building sample; combine them in a logical fashion while preserving the ethnographic validity of each individual decision model. Preserving the ethnographic validity of each individual decision model means that the informants still have to "go down" the path of the tree that they went down before and wind up at the same outcome where they wound up before. It does not necessarily mean that the "emic" features of each decision criterion in each individual decision tree are preserved; it is often necessary to generalize "emic" decision criteria of several individuals into one criterion which may be so general that it appears "etic." The generalized etic criterion, however, should include the individual emic criteria as its special cases which could be listed. As in the last step, there is more than one way to combine/juggle decision criteria in a tree model, and the only way to see which model is the better model is to subject them both to empirical testing in the next chapter. But now, let's look at two methods to combine criteria in a tree model.

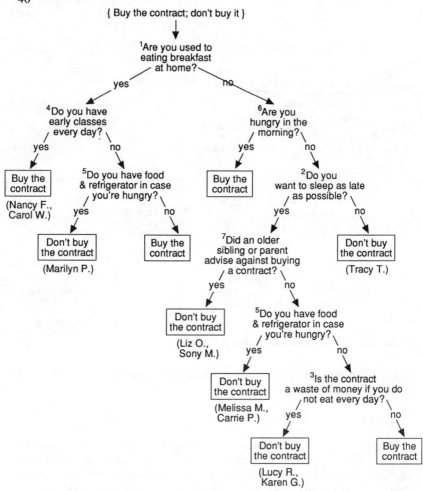

Figure 2.7 Composite Model₁ of the Freshman's Decision to Buy or Not Buy a Breakfast Contract

One method is an ad hoc method, in which you juggle decision criteria "by the seat of your pants" and see if the tree you get makes sense and predicts well enough. Figure 2.7 is an example of a tree you'd get if you used this method, and it's not a bad model of the breakfast contract decision. The logic of the model is twofold. On the left-hand path, students buy the breakfast contract if they're used to eating breakfast at home and have early classes everyday. On the right-hand path, students don't buy the breakfast contract if they're not used to eating breakfast at home, are not hungry in the morning, want to sleep as late as possible, and either have an older sibling who advised them against the contract, or have food and a refrigerator in case they're hungry, or think the contract is a waste of money if they don't eat breakfast every day. This makes sense.

Well, you might say, what's wrong with it? It predicts what these 10 informants do! My problem with this tree is that it could be more logically constructed. The way to do that is to first look at the decision criteria and identify the *reasons* for the informant to do X, e.g., for a student to get a breakfast contract. Second, identify the main branches of the tree that lead to each outcome (in this case, "Buy the contract" and "Don't buy it"), and label one branch the *Buy the contract unless*... branch and the other *Don't Buy the contract unless*... branch. Third, identify the "unless-conditions" or constraints on each branch that cause the decision maker to back off from that choice and pick the other alternative. Fourth, stand back and see if the new tree is logical and complete. Fifth, see if the informants still "go down" the path of the tree that they went down before, i.e., still pass the criteria they passed before, although maybe not in the same order, and wind up at the same outcome where they wound up before. Let's go over these steps which produce Figure 2.8, a much more logical model of the breakfast contract decision.

STEPS 8.1–8.2.

Look at the decision criteria in the individual tree models and identify the reasons students want a breakfast contract. A glance at Figures 2.1 to 2.6 shows at least three criteria that are good reasons to want a breakfast contract: (1) "Are you used to eating breakfast at home?" (6) "Are you hungry in the morning?" and (8) "Have early classes and feel you need three good meals/day?" Any one of these reasons should lead a student to the outcome "Buy a breakfast contract" if there are no constraints blocking the contract option.

In general, if we use the convention that "yes" answers take the left-hand path and "no" answers take the right-hand path, as in:

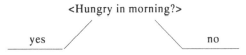

then the reasons for a decision maker to buy the contract (or do X in the {Do X; don't} decision) usually come at the top of the tree and form a right-branching tree, as in Figure 2.9. Note that any one reason is sufficient to lead the decision maker to the command "Do X unless. . . ." The constraints to the option "Do X" — what I refer to as the "unless conditions" because the decision maker does X unless one or more of

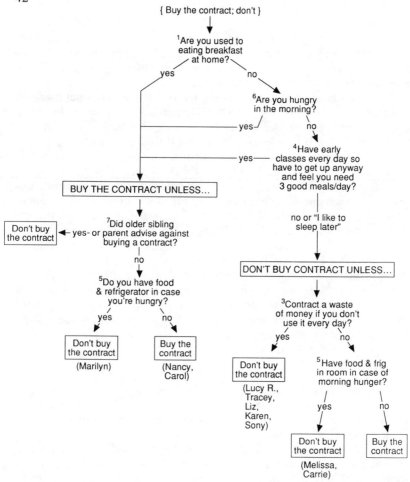

Figure 2.8 Composite Model$_2$ of the Freshman's Decision to Buy or Not Buy a Breakfast Contract

these constraints holds — come next logically. We thus first list the reasons to do X, and then list the constraints to prevent the decision maker from doing X. The constraints also form a right-branching tree under the command, "Do X unless. . . ." The right-branching form of the constraints can be seen in Figure 2.10.

In a typical {Do it; don't do it} decision, this should be the logical form of the decision tree: reasons for doing the action come first, constraints preventing the action second. Again note that any one reason is sufficient to lead the decision maker to the command midway down

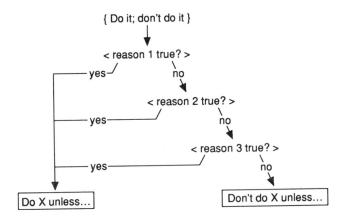

Figure 2.9 Reasons in a "Do It; Don't Do It" Decision

the tree, "Do X unless" . . . (the following constraints are true); while any one constraint is sufficient to *stop* the decision maker from doing X. You don't have to have all the reasons in the world to do something, but you have to pass all the constraints in order to do it. Also note that "Don't do X" also has its own set of constraints: there's an unless-condition or exception to every rule, as Harris (1974) has correctly pointed out.

STEP 8.3.

Identify the "unless-conditions" or constraints on each branch that cause the decision maker to pick the other alternative. Another glance at Figures 2.1 to 2.6 lets us identify the conditions that block students from getting a breakfast contract. They include: (5) "Do you have food and refrigerator in case you're hungry?" and (7) "Did an older sibling or parent advise against buying a contract?" These constraints are thus unless conditions that belong under the reasons to get a breakfast contract in the composite decision tree in Figure 2.8.

STEP 8.4.

Stand back and see if the new tree is logical and complete. Does the new tree have an internal logic of its own? Have you covered all the logical possibilities of aspects and alternatives that informants can use? Note that in the revised model in Figure 2.8, criterion 2, "Do you want to sleep as late as possible?" is now missing; whereas criterion 5, "Do

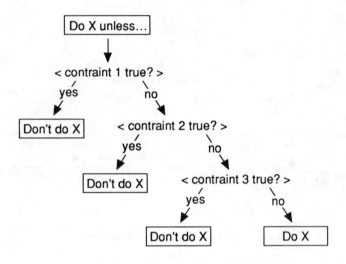

Figure 2.10 Constraints in a "Do It; Don't Do It" Decision

you have food and refrigerator in case you're hungry?" is still repeated twice, on both branches of the tree. Why? Criterion 2 is the logical opposite or the "no" response to criterion 4, "Have early classes every day so have to get up anyway and feel you need 3 good meals/day?" Logically, one either gets up early or one sleeps late and misses breakfast, and then the contract is a waste of money. This logic eliminates criterion 2 from the tree; or put another way, criterion 4 now represents the student's prior decision process to be a morning person and get up versus a night person and sleep late. Criterion 5, "Do you have food and refrigerator in case you're hungry?" on the other hand, is still needed on both branches of the tree because it is the logical alternative to buying a breakfast contract. If one is an active college student and does not buy a breakfast contract, one had better have the alternative of handy food available to munch on.

STEP 8.5.

See if the new tree is still empirically correct and the informants still "go down" the path of the tree that they went down before. Informants in the model-building sample should still pass criteria they passed before you rearranged the model in a more logical form, although maybe not in the same order, and should wind up at the same outcome where they wound up before. One wants a tree model as logical as possible. But more than logical, it should be as predictive of choices of this sample as is possible because if it doesn't predict choices of the model-building sample, it will not predict the decisions of the model-testing sample or the population very well either. "Putting an informant's (data) down the tree" requires the modeler to have asked each informant all the questions representing all the criteria on the path they (i.e., their data) proceed down. This is quite difficult if only one interview is conducted with the first informants interviewed; hence it is important to return to these first people and ask them about the criteria identified by the last informants interviewed. It is also the reason why I prefer the indirect method of eliciting decision criteria in step 7. When one builds the composite decision tree and questionnaire at the same time, simultaneously identifying criteria and adding questions to the questionnaire, one is not only preparing for the test of the decision model described in the next chapter, but one also has a better grasp of what criteria each informant has actually passed. No matter which method you use to build the model, however, the direct or the indirect, you can end up with the same result, a composite model (or models) to be tested in Chapter 3.

Homework 2.4: Interview ten informants, five who go to McDonald's for lunch and five who don't. Use the direct method on the first five informants and model their decisions. Now use the indirect method on the last five informants to build a composite model of the decision to go to McDonald's for lunch. Now revise your complete model following the steps in step 8.

3. HOW TO TEST DECISION MODELS

This chapter describes how to test a decision model. It starts with a simple "Do it; don't do it" decision model, such as the breakfast contract decision, and develops a questionnaire to test that decision. It explains how to know when the model you've built is failing during the test interviews, what to do when an error occurs, and how to "backtrack" to find out *why* an informant is an error of your model in the sense that his or her behavior is unexplained by the model. If you are not doing your own personal interviews to test the model, it presents an alternative strategy. Finally, it describes how to devise and test an alternative model which might predict better than the original composite model. Revising the first composite model entails juggling constraints or paths around and/or adding a constraint(s) or path(s). Examples of test decisions include the breakfast contract decision and farmers' decisions to get credit for fertilizer in Malawi.

Once a decision model is "built" or programmed, based on interviews with a first sample of decision makers, it should be tested for accuracy in predicting other choice data. Like any model, there is no point to building it unless one also tests it, to see how good a representation of reality it really is. The test stage is necessary for a *predictive* study, which attempts to predict actual choice behavior of individuals in a group, as opposed to a merely *descriptive* study, which describes how some choices were historically made in the group. The test or validation stage has two requirements. First, the model built using the steps outlined in Chapter 2 cannot be further modified or "fiddled with." If it is modified, it becomes descriptive, and a new validation/*test* must ensue. Second, informants used in the model building stage should *not* be included in validation testing; another set of informants are used to test the model.

If you've worked through (not just read) the logic of the individual and composite trees of Chapter 2 and built your own first decision model, you are now ready to test your decision model with choice data collected from another sample of decision makers from the same population or group. How can you do this? As in Chapter 2, we can think of the process of model testing as one of following a plan which has well-defined steps, like the steps in a recipe. They are the following.

STEP 1.

Make up a formal questionnaire to test the composite model you've already developed, using each decision criterion as a question in a questionnaire. The questions in this questionnaire are no longer open-ended, as were the questions in the model-building phase of the research; now they are simply yes/no questions which elicit informants' yes/no responses used to test the model. Note that informants' responses and not the researcher's judgment about whether informants use the specified decision rules are used to test the model; this helps prevent bias and "fudging the data" by the researcher. It also produces *errors* if the informant does not hear or understand the question properly or misinterprets the question. The resulting error rate tells us how well the model predicts.

Table 3.1 shows the questionnaire developed by Karen Rain to test the breakfast contract decision. It is simply a list of the questions made from the decision criteria of the composite model that was built in step 7, Chapter 2. If you have used the indirect method of building your decision model of the decision to go to McDonald's for lunch, you've already started this questionnaire before the interview with the second informant, and all you have to do is finish it. If you haven't already started the questionnaire because you believe in more open-ended interviews and you have chosen the direct method of model building,

Table 3.1 A Questionnaire for the Breakfast Contract Decision

(A) **FACTUAL QUESTIONS**	
(1) Did you buy the breakfast contract this freshman year?	yes_____ no_____
(B) **DECISION CRITERIA:**	
(1) Are you used to eating breakfast at home?	yes_____ no_____
(2) Do you want to sleep as late as possible?	yes_____ no_____
(3) Is the contract a waste of money if you do not eat every day?	yes_____ no_____
(4) Do you have early classes every day?	yes_____ no_____
(5) Do you have food and refrigerator in case you are hungry?	yes_____ no_____
(6) Are you hungry in the morning?	yes_____ no_____
(7) Did an older sibling or parent advise against buying a contract?	yes_____ no_____
(8) Do you have early classes every day and feel you need three good meals a day?	yes_____ no_____

then it's time now to turn every criterion in the composite model into a question, as in Table 3.1.

STEP 2.

As you did in step 5 of Chapter 2, decide on a sample of decision makers to use to test your model. Decide when and where to interview them. To provide a true test of the model, none of the original informants should be included in this test sample. As in step 5 of Chapter 2, you should select a sample that's as representative as possible of the population of people who make the decision, e.g., freshmen who do and don't buy the breakfast contract and people who go and don't go to McDonald's for lunch. Again, the size of the validation sample depends on whether the population is a relatively homogeneous group in one "cultural scene," in which case a sample size of 25 to 30 might do. If you are doing a study of five homogeneous groups or a regional study of five agroclimatic zones, a sample size of 125 to 150 may be necessary. Remember that you want to capture as much variation as possible in your sample, and a decision study is unlike other studies aimed at gathering quantitative data representative of the population because you need *two test subsamples* to test your model. The first subsample are people who, in fact, "do it"; they are necessary to test the reasons for "doing it" (e.g., buying the breakfast contract, going to the restaurant). The second subsample of people who "don't do it" are also needed to test the constraints which prevent these people from doing it.

STEP 3.

Also elicit quantitative data about what the informant is actually doing so that you know what choice is really made *before* you ask the informant questions about why he or she is making that choice. In Table 3.1, the "quantitative" data is just question A1, "Did you buy the contract?" In a more complicated model of the same decision, however, quantitative data might also include the price of the breakfast contract, the price of a refrigerator (rental and/or total purchase price), and the cost of keeping food in the room, as well as question A1. The quantitative part of the questionnaire can get as detailed as you need in order to get an accurate picture of what the informant is actually doing.

Homework 3.1: Note that price and cost criteria do not appear in the breakfast contract decision models of Chapter 2; apparently freshmen in this residence hall at this Ivy-League university did not worry about having the money either for the breakfast contract or their own refrigerator. Price and cost, therefore, were not decision criteria for them. The omission of these criteria, however, may mean that this decision model is not valid for freshmen at another university, for whom money might be more of a problem. How would you test this hypothesis at your university? What would price and cost criteria look like in your model?

STEP 4.

During the test interviews, know when the model you've built is failing and identify the errors of the model. You can do this if you do the test interviews yourself and you know the decision model so well that red lights flash — and warning bells sound — in your brain when an error occurs during an interview. In the past, I've done this by working and reworking the tree model until it's almost memorized. Then I keep the tree model in perceptual short-term memory and also get very familiar with the questionnaire by practicing on informants before I start on the test sample. After five informants are interviewed, I have both tree model and questionnaire practically memorized, and know when the person I'm interviewing is an "error" of the model. Of course, the informant is never in error; instead, it's the model that's in error for not being able to explain the choice behavior of the informant.

What should you do when the decision model is failing? Should you correct an informant — or subtly try to point out the inconsistencies in his or her different replies at different parts of the questionnaire? No, never. That is tantamount to asking a leading question. Again, the problem with leading or correcting informants is that they usually are eager to please and tend to agree with you rather than contradict you. By leading them, you have lost the information you desperately wanted. Instead, at the *end* of the questionnaire you should *backtrack,* i.e., revert to open-ended questions again to find out why your model has failed to predict why this particular informant did what he or she did and is therefore an "error" of the model — in the sense that his or her behavior is unexplained by the model.

For example, in the breakfast contract decision, you might simply ask, "Well, if you are used to eating breakfast at home, and want to sleep as late as possible, and you consider the contract a waste of money if you do not eat everyday, but you ended up getting the breakfast contract, why did you?" This question may elicit a new if-condition leading to the outcome, "Buy the contract." In fact, this is exactly what happened when Karen Rain tested Figure 2.7 on 10 more freshmen who both did and did not buy breakfast contracts; these results are shown in Figure 3.1.

STEP 5.

After the test interviews, calculate the error rate (and success rate) of your model(s). In Figure 3.1 of the breakfast contract decision, the model makes an error if it predicts the student buys a breakfast contract but she does not *or* if it predicts the student does not buy a contract but she does. In the simplest test of the model, errors are counted on each path and a simple "success rate" for the model is calculated by dividing the total number of successes by the total number of cases. If the decision model successfully predicts 85-90% of the choices of the individuals in the group, it is assumed to be an adequate model of the individual decision process for that group of individuals. Karen's results in Figure 3.1 show a prediction rate of 60%, which is very low for tree models; but her results also allow us to identify the errors of the model: Carole M., Mary F., Ann C., and Barb B.

But what if someone else has been testing your models for you, either in person or on the phone, and you can discover the errors only after it's too late to backtrack? In this case, put the questionnaires of the "errors" together in one pile, and go over the statements of the informants. If you've taped the interviews, listen to the errors' tapes again. Ask yourself: "What do they have in common? Is there a pattern here?"

STEP 6.

Listen to what "the errors" say about why they do what they do, and devise an alternative model to predict their choices, by (a) rephrasing or generalizing an existing criterion, or (b) adding another criterion, or (c) switching the order of criteria or even whole paths of the tree.

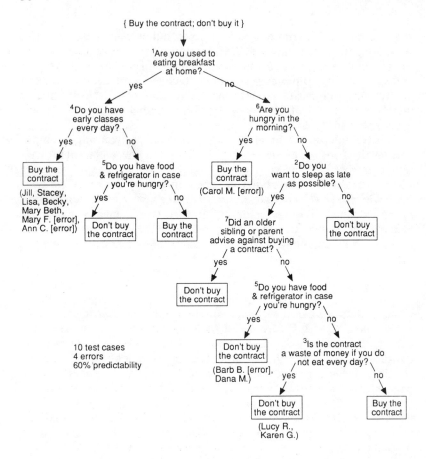

Figure 3.1 Composite Model₁ of the Freshman's Decision to Buy or Not Buy a Breakfast Contract

After you make these changes, however, be sure that the previous "successes" of the model continue to be successes. Note that this part of the model-revising process gets to be pretty nitty-gritty as the researcher judges, "Well, now we predict Mary; is Bob still okay?"

Example One: Testing the Breakfast Contract Decision

As a first example of this part of the methodology, let's look at profiles of "the errors" in the college freshman's breakfast contract decision. Carole M. did not buy a contract. The political science major from Missouri said that although she was hungry in the morning, she did not want to get up early to eat. Since she has late classes, Carole prefers to make her own breakfast in her room at her own convenience and has a refrigerator in her room. Before coming to school, she was not used to having breakfast in the morning. Mary F. also did not buy a contract. The College of Arts and Sciences student from Connecticut always had breakfast at home, but she felt that she would prefer to sleep later in the morning instead of getting up to eat. Even though she does have early classes, Mary is not always hungry, so she keeps food and a refrigerator in her room and makes her own breakfast on the occasions when she is hungry.

Ann C., an audiology major in the School of Speech who comes from Michigan, did not buy a contract because she forgot to send in the necessary forms. She was used to eating breakfast at home but did not know if she would get up in time for breakfast every morning. She thought that it would be just as easy to prepare something in her own room, and she had a refrigerator.

Barb B. did buy a contract, but for a reason not encountered in the first model-building sample. (Note the dangers of having too small a sample with which to build your model!) The College of Arts and Sciences student from Oklahoma stated that her father had insisted that she have a contract even though she did not want one. Barb said that she is not hungry in the morning, is not used to eating breakfast at home, likes to sleep as late as possible in the morning, and does keep breakfast foods in her room.

Is there a common pattern running through any of the responses of these freshmen? Yes: What Mary F., Ann C., and Carole M. have in common is breakfast food in their room and their desire for the convenience of eating breakfast in their own room when they want. In fact, after the ten test interviews, Karen Rain felt that the convenience of eating breakfast in one's room was a more important constraint to breakfast contracts than the need to sleep late in the morning. Therefore, we add to Figure 3.2 another criterion 8, "Like the convenience of eating in your room when you want?" which is logically prior to criterion 5, "Have food & frig . . . ," because students wouldn't bother with food and refrigerators in their rooms unless they wanted more convenience. Now are these "errors" predicted by the revised model in Figure 3.2 any better than they were by the original model in Figure 3.1? Yes, their choices are now predicted by Figure 3.2. All three girls are hungry in the morning or are used to eating breakfast, so they go down the left-hand "Buy the contract unless . . ." path in Figure 3.2; but all get blocked from buying the contract at criteria 8 and 5 and so don't buy a breakfast contract. The alternative model in Figure 3.2 now predicts 90% of the test cases, and so is a better model than that of Figure 3.1.

52

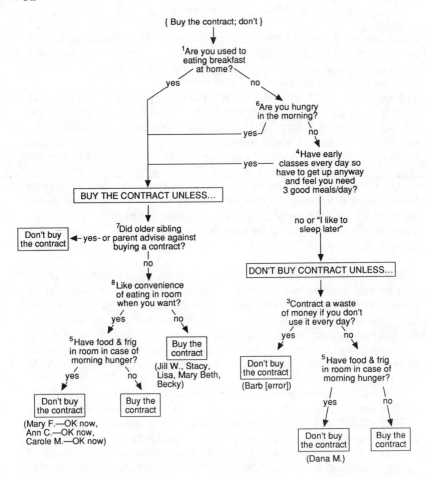

Figure 3.2 Composite Model$_2$ of the freshman's Decision to Buy or Not Buy a Breakfast Contract

But Barb B.'s choice is still unexplained by both models in Figures 3.1 and 3.2. We could, however, revise Figure 3.2 by adding a new criterion 10, as an unless-condition on the "Don't buy the contract" path: "Did your parents insist you buy the breakfast contract?" The danger in adding this new criterion to the model of Figure 3.2 is that it may be an *idiosyncratic* decision criterion, i.e., one that is capable of predicting only a very small number of the test cases. If this is the case, it would be better to leave Barb B. as an error of the model in order to have a *parsimonious* model, i.e., a model with the smallest number of decision criteria — so that *The Thing* does not take over. (In Chapter 5, we will see some complicated models that carry the risk of becoming like *The Thing.*) This is thus another *decision* that you, the researcher, have to make in order to build and test decision models. Do you want a tree as parsimonious as possible, and will you accept one with a lower success rate; *or* do you want one as predictive as possible, and will you accept a lot of possibly idiosyncratic decision criteria?

STEP 7.

After devising an alternative model which might predict better than the original composite model, test the alternative model with the test sample data, and compare the two models. The rationale behind this step comes from Lave and March (1975) who rightly state that because any model is a representation of reality, the only test of a model is whether it is better or worse than another model or representation. Because a model predicts 90% of the choice data of the test cases does not mean that it is "the real, actual model" of the decision in question; this is a contradiction in terms. Indeed, there might be a better (more parsimonious) model that can predict 95% of the same choice data. Your job as a modeler is thus to present your model and report on its performance (its success rate and number of criteria). If you can also show that it's better than an alternative model, go for it! This step is relatively easy to do if the changes made in the composite models are merely changes in the ordering of criteria or paths of the tree. In this case, if an informant is asked every question on the questionnaire, no matter which path he or she seems to be following, then you already have every informant's responses to use to test the new model.

Testing the alternative model is a bit harder if the changes made in the original composite model are additions of new decision criteria (like criterion 8 in our example) which were not posed as questions on the questionnaire. In this case, the *test* phase should then be repeated on a new, independent test sample because the most important part of validation is that the model isn't "fiddled with." If the model is modified, we have returned to the model-building phase of Chapter 2 and are no longer in the test phase of the research. The model has become a *descriptive* and not a *predictive* model because criteria have been modified to best fit this sample. Oftentimes, however, the researcher doesn't have time to interview another test sample, and he or she may already know the answers to the new questions for the original test sample from reviewing the informants' responses to the questionnaire or listening again to the taped interviews. The researcher may then decide to rely on this knowledge rather than resample. In the latter case, the researcher runs the risk of fudging the data and ending up with a descriptive rather than predictive alternative decision model.

Homework 3.2: In the breakfast contract decision, we found that Figure 3.2 predicts 90% of the test cases, whereas Figure 3.1 predicted only 60% of the same cases, and so Figure 3.2 is a better model. Follow the steps outlined in this chapter and develop a questionnaire to test your composite model of the lunch-at-McDonald's decision. Then identify the errors of model$_1$ and develop and test an alternative model$_2$. Which model predicts better? Which is more parsimonious?

Example Two: Testing the African Farmer's Credit Decision

For the second example of the testing method, let's return to the model of the Malawi farmer's credit decision in Figures 1.3 and 1.4 which, unfortunately, was built with a small sample of only nine decision makers.[5] It was then tested with data from 30 additional farmers who lived in different locations scattered over three districts: Lilongwe, Kasungu, and Salima. Although farmers in this sample were on the average bigger, more experienced farmers than is the norm (with average landholdings of 3.02 ha.), in other respects the sample is fairly representative of Malawi smallholders.[6] The model originally tested failed to predict the choices of six farmers, for a success rate of only 85%.

Since this is a poor success rate for decision tree models, I looked for a pattern in the model's failures. The pattern was clear: The model failed to predict the choices of six women household heads, five of whom had less than two acres.[7] The failures showed up at the risk-minimization criteria. These women said they would not join a credit club because of "the way they get money back"; but that yes, hunger was more dangerous and risky than their not being able to repay credit for fertilizer and, yes, not applying fertilizer on local maize invited low yields and the risk of hunger. The model thus predicts that these women should get credit for fertilizer but they don't because it's too risky. The mistake in the model, called model$_1$, is: the risk of not repaying credit is such an important constraint that it doesn't belong at the bottom of the tree in stage 2 but should be higher up the tree in stage 1, the elimination stage, where it can eliminate any possibility of women joining a credit club. To solve this problem in model$_2$, *criterion 5 was generalized* (step 6a) to cover not only the special case of women who had never had loans before and so wouldn't take the risks of large fertilizer loans but also to handle the cases of women farmers who, for various reasons (e.g., someone else's previous bad experience with a credit club when they couldn't repay), wouldn't take the risks of not being able to repay the loan.

Another way the original model$_1$ was incorrect was in being too optimistic. It did not allow for the fact that the smallest smallholders might feel hopeless in their poverty, and this would cause them to not even *ask* to join a credit club and thus get the fertilizer and produce the maize to get them out of their impoverished condition.[8] Such was the

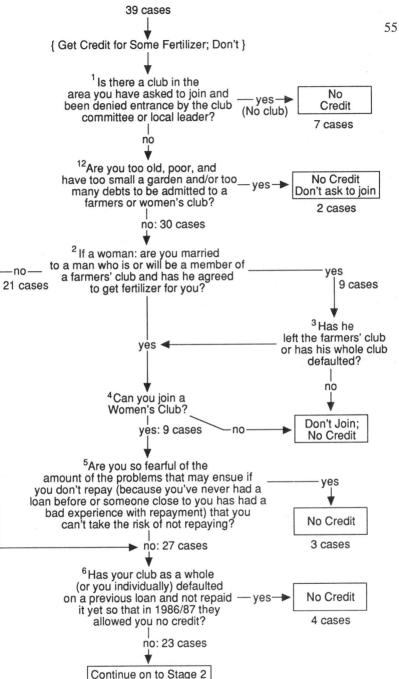

Figure 3.3 Stage One of the Malawi Farmer's Decision To Get Credit for Some Fertilizer Via a Farmers' or Women's Club

56

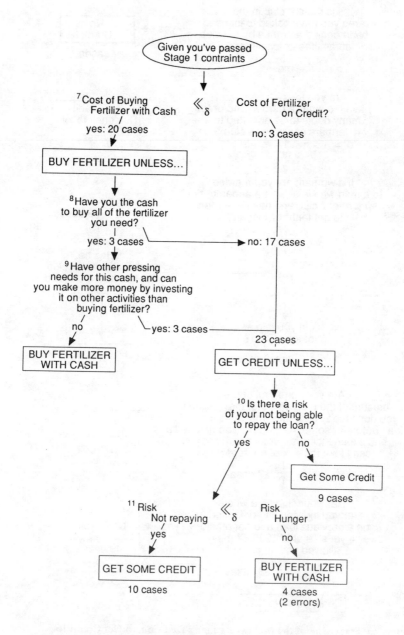

Figure 3.4 Stage Two of the Malawi Farmer's Credit Decision

situation of at least two women household heads: They weren't denied entrance to a club in criterion 1 because they felt their case for admission to the club was so hopeless that they didn't even ask to join. To correct for this error of $model_1$, *criterion 12 was added* (step 6b) in the elimination stage of $model_2$, where it rapidly eliminates the smallholder who feels too old, poor, or small to join a credit club and so doesn't ask. Given these two revisions to $model_1$, $model_2$ in Figures 3.3 and 3.4 now describes 95% of the farmers' choices. Note that $model_2$ is termed a descriptive rather than predictive model because I did not have the time to properly test $model_2$ on a new independent sample of decision makers after adding criterion 12. Ideally, this new test should be done in order to compare the two alternative models.

Given this example of how to generalize a narrow decision criterion (step 6a), how to add new decision criteria (step 6b), and how to build and compare alternative decision models (step 7), we can now move on to other questions. One such question is: Of what use for government planners is this knowledge of how an admittedly small sample of farmers makes credit decisions? We return to answer this question in Chapter 6 because next on our agenda is a discussion of "what not to do" and "what to do when you've done it."

4. HOW NOT TO DO IT: COMMON PROBLEMS

This chapter describes how to recognize and correct some common errors that decision-tree modelers make when building and testing their first models. It explains what to do when a tree model is just a simple checklist or tangly "vine," when your informant gets ambiguous or suddenly chooses a new and unanticipated outcome, or when no errors appear at the testing stage. It describes how to recognize an error when you see one. It also describes the ordering aspect, a "circular" criterion that can't predict, and an if-condition when your informant says "It depends."

What can you do when you run into modeling and testing problems? As with computer programming problems and errors, the easiest thing to do is to see if other people have had the same problems before and find out how they solved them. In this Chapter, we review some of these common problems and errors of decision tree modelers and suggest possible solutions.

Common Problem #1: A Simplistic Model

As mentioned in Chapter 2, during your very first model-building interview you can make your first mistake, which is to build a model

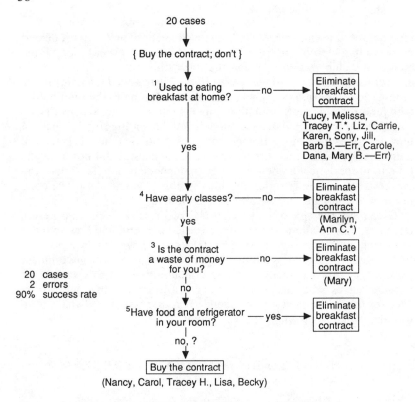

Figure 4.1 A Too-Simple "Elimination-by-Aspects" Model of the Freshman's Breakfast Contract Decision Process

which is just too simple to be a good model of an informant's logical decision process. In the breakfast contract decision, for example, you could have listened to Lucy's explanation of why she didn't buy the breakfast contract and recognized only the first criterion, "Are you used to eating breakfast at home?" as a decision criterion. Let's assume that you have already put this criterion in the model of Figure 2.1b. You now go on to the second informant, Nancy, and elicit from her only one decision criterion 4, "Do you have early classes every day." After interviews with ten informants, you might end up with the four aspects in Figure 4.1, which seem to predict the choices of your 20 informants accurately. Note that this model can also be represented by a checklist because it's a simple straight-line "elimination-by-aspects" model, which is usually the first stage of a real-life decision process.

This new model looks very concise and predicts decisions of 90% of Karen Rain's sample of freshmen at Northwestern. What's wrong with it? According to Chapter 2, a decision model should be *both logical and predictive* of choices made in real life by real people (steps 8.4 and 8.5). Correspondingly, the test of a decision model is whether it predicts most informants' decisions based on what *they* claim *their* decision criteria are. Decision criteria should thus contain *"emic"* categories, i.e., units of meaning drawn from the culture bearers themselves, which can be contrasted with *"etic"* categories, which may have meaning for outside observers of a culture but need not have meaning for the people of the specific culture under study (Harris, 1979: 32).

Unfortunately, the model in Figure 4.1 cannot live up to these standards. It can predict choices made by freshmen students, but not according to what they claim their decision criteria are. In the case of Tracey T., for example, criterion 1 sends her to the "Eliminate the contract" option, which is what she did, but not for the reason given in criterion 1. Similarly, criterion 4 sends Ann C. to eliminate the contract, but not for the reason stated. These two cases are not errors of the model because it does predict the choices they made. However, the model does not capture their logical processes because it's just too simple; its prediction rate is due to spurious correlation.

Because the model is so simple, the first criterion at the top of the tree does most (12) of the predicting of the (15) "Don't buy the contract" cases and also makes all of the (two) errors in the model. This is because the informants look at other decision criteria only if they say yes to criterion 1. The model thus does not allow decision makers to look at combinations of decision criteria; for this reason, it is too restrictive a model of real-life decisions, in contrast to the model in Figure 3.2.

Unfortunately, many first-time decision modelers produce such an oversimplified stage-one model. How can you avoid this problem? One way is to *probe further* when an informant gives you only one simple decision criterion, like criterion 1.[9] Ask, "Well, how does that affect whether or not you get the breakfast contract? Under what other circumstances might you decide to buy a breakfast contract?" For similar reasons, don't stop, but probe further if your informant says she doesn't get the contract because "it would be a waste of money for her parents," criterion 3. Ask why. You would then probably elicit other criteria and develop a tree with combinations of criteria rather than a simple string of single, unrelated criteria.

Another way to find combinations of criteria is to listen for the words "it depends" coming from informants. Make red lights flash in your brain when you hear these words, because they mean an if-condition or decision criterion is about to come out of your informant's mouth. For example, the ethnographer asks, "Do you fertilize at planting if you plant maize on *barrial* soils?" Informant: "It depends." Ethnographer: "On what?" Informant: "On whether the 'regular' rains come in mid-

combinations of criteria

May or early June." Now the ethnographer knows that one key to fertilizing at planting is the date that the "regular" rains come, as well as the soil type. He or she can turn the informant's answer into a decision criterion, "Did the 'regular' rains come in mid-May or early June this year?" This criterion will fit into a combination of criteria with "Do you plant maize on *'barrial'* soils?" and a tree will result (Gladwin, 1979).

Common Problem #2: Ambiguous Informants

This solution reminds me of another problem, that of the informant who doesn't like yes/no answers or who can't answer yes/no to certain questions. "Do you want to sleep as late as possible in the morning?" "Sometimes." "Is the contract a waste of money if you do not eat every day?" "Well, . . . maybe; it depends." Should this informant be dumped or assigned a yes/no response by fiat? No, never. This informant is to be treasured, stroked, *listened to,* and questioned further—but gently. This informant is not really a problem but *a find!* You, the ethnographer, want to find out what's wrong with your model; that's your aim. When you find an ambiguous informant, you're halfway there, because, if you gently probe further, your informant will tell you what's wrong with your model. He or she will tell you the criterion that's missing from your model, or the order that you haven't gotten straight yet, or the individual variation that you haven't picked up yet, for whatever reason. So, stay in your seat, although red lights are flashing in your brain and warning bells are going off, and quietly ask for the if-condition. "Well, when do you want to sleep as late as possible — and when don't you?" "Well, when is the contract a waste of money — and when isn't it?" Get ready to hear another decision criterion.

Common Problem #3: Circular Criteria

Many students use circular criteria in their first models, or criteria that can't predict outcomes or choices because they ask the decision maker if they want one particular outcome over another. An example is "Would you prefer to eat breakfast in your own room at your convenience on a regular basis?" What's wrong with this? *The informant's preference regarding where breakfast is eaten is exactly what we want to predict,* based on the informant's "score" on independent variables or, in this case, decision criteria.[10] We thus cannot phrase criteria so that they have the outcome *within* them or depend on the outcome; we should phrase criteria so that they are *independent* of the outcome, e.g., "Do you like the convenience of eating in your own room on a regular basis?" or "Is the convenience of eating in your own room, when you want, important to you?" The latter phrasing of the above criterion is open-ended and focuses on convenience as an independent variable, which, depending on the informant's reply, may lead either to the "Buy the contract" outcome or the "Don't buy the breakfast contract" outcome. Other examples of circular criteria include: Did you pick this restaurant because you were in a hurry? Did you eat at the restaurant because of the senior citizen's discount? Did you pick this restaurant because it fit your budget? In contrast, these criteria should be: Are (or were) you in a hurry? Can you get a senior citizen's discount at restaurant X? Do (or did) your friends want to go to restaurant X? Does it fit your budget?

Common Problem #4: No Errors

Oftentimes, students turn up with a perfect model, i.e., they do not find a single informant whose choice their model fails to predict. Subsequently, I'm suspicious because *every model is an imperfect representation* of the real world, just as the most sophisticated toy train is an imperfect representation of a real train. A decision model is particularly imperfect because some decision makers are apt to use idiosyncratic criteria that are hard to elicit from a small model-building sample because they are infrequently used.

What can you do if you fail to find one error of your model? (Yes, you have them.) Maybe you're not recognizing the cases that are errors because your informants seem so logical when you interview them that you think your equally logical model should predict them. Maybe you want your brainchild of a model to be so good that, during the interview, you let a few cases slide by a few criteria that are not really *general* enough to account for them. Maybe an informant answers "yes" to a question during the interview that you think should have been a "no" based on other data, and you probe further until he or she changes the answer. No fair: This is leading! But, you say, the informant misinterpreted the question. Agreed, and so this is an error.

For these reasons, a computerized test is superior to one which puts informants' data down the tree with pencil and paper. In its absence, you have to simulate a computer, and, with the questionnaires from the test sample and each informant's responses to the questions as stated in the questionnaire, put the informant "down the tree." Then compare the informant's actual choice with what the tree predicts the informant should have chosen. If the actual choice and the tree do not agree, you have an error. Even with a computerized test, it is easy to "fudge" during the test interviews by not asking decision-criteria questions exactly as phrased in the tree or questionnaire and by letting informants slide around them. For this reason, the person administering the test questionnaire has to be rigorous and disciplined and have a scientific attitude toward errors.[11]

Common Problem #5: The Model Is a Vine, Not a Tree

Of all the problems encountered by the uninitiated tree modeler, this is the most common. The student listens to a lot of decision "episodes" or stories about why and when and how the informants did X and elicits very detailed decision criteria and puts them all verbatim into a tree, which then turns into a long, windy vine. Let's assume that you have produced the "vine" in Figures 4.2–4.3 as your model of the decision to go to McDonald's for lunch. (This tree is actually the product of two students of the 1988 NSF Summer Methods Institute who were also assigned the decision to go to McDonald's for lunch as homework. They prefer to remain anonymous but have graciously let me use their vine.) There's nothing empirically wrong with this vine, and there's a lot of good episodic information in it; but, aesthetically, it is ugly, and it goes on and on.

What can be done to turn this vine into a proper decision tree with beautiful branches? *First, generalize some of the criteria, i.e., combine them to eliminate redundancy; second, cluster the decision criteria logically; third, identify and eliminate decision criteria that belong in a logically prior (or later) decision, and put them in another tree.*

The first and easiest way to shorten a vine is to put similar criteria together into one general criteria. In Figures 4.2–4.3, the two knowledge constraints 14 and 16 can be generalized into one criterion (3) in Figure 4.4. Similarly, criteria 6 (the Happy Meal case), criterion 7 (the games case), and criterion 5 (the case of the companion's choice) can be put into one general criterion, "[2]Have you agreed to let your companion choose the restaurant?" in Figure 4.4. Presumably, criteria 6 and 7 are aspects in the decisions of children who are luncheon companions. They and not the informant are making the decision this time; and the Happy Meal and games are "something special McDonald's has to offer them that they crave," and so don't belong in the informant's decision process at all. In these two cases, the informant will say "yes" to criterion 2 in Figure 4.4, and so exit the model; while the informant's children will proceed down their decision trees to criterion 8, answer "yes," and they'll all go to McDonald's for lunch.

Analogously, the convenience criterion 4, the fast service criteria 3 and 11, and the predictability criterion 8 can all be summarized in criterion 7 in Figure 4.4. These features of a fast-food restaurant chain are put together in criterion 7 because they are inseparable: With convenience of location and speed of service comes the inevitable homogeneity (and predictability) of the restaurant chain's products.

A vine can also be made more treelike by juxtaposing criteria that fit together logically, e.g., criteria that enable one to get to McDonald's such as transportation, time, money, and knowledge. These "enabling" criteria 3, 4, 5, and 6 are juxtaposed in stage 1 of the decision in

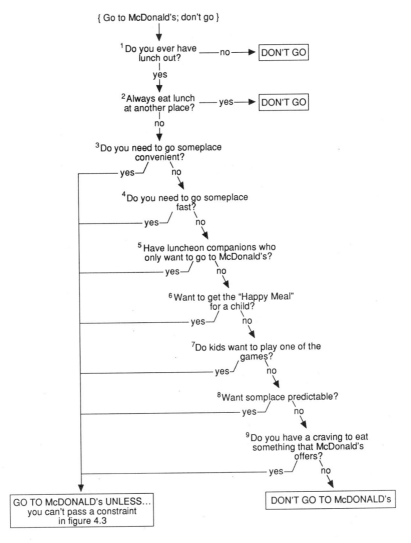

Figure 4.2 Student's Model of the Decision to Go to McDonald's for Lunch

Figure 4.4. Then comes the ordering aspect that is "maximized" in this decision: convenience and predictability of a fast-food place. This aspect signals the start of stage 2, the hard-core part of the decision process. But, as we claim below, this is obscured in a simple {Go to X; don't go} decision in which the decision maker chooses between going to X versus not going at all. In this kind of decision, all aspects — even

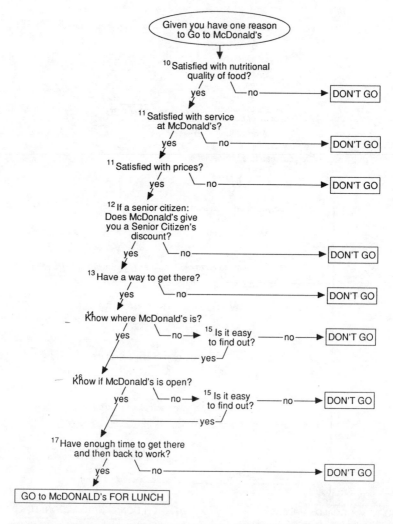

Figure 4.3 Constraints in Student's Model of Decision to Go to McDonald's for Lunch

the ordering aspect — end up as constraints which must be passed. If the decision maker *needs* convenient, predictable, fast food and can pass the stage-two constraint of food-quality or nutrition (criterion 9), then McDonald's is chosen. If convenience is not needed today, but the decision maker has a craving for something McDonald's offers (criterion 8), e.g., a Big Mac or a Happy Meal, and he or she can pass the nutrition constraint, then McDonald's is chosen again. (Note that there

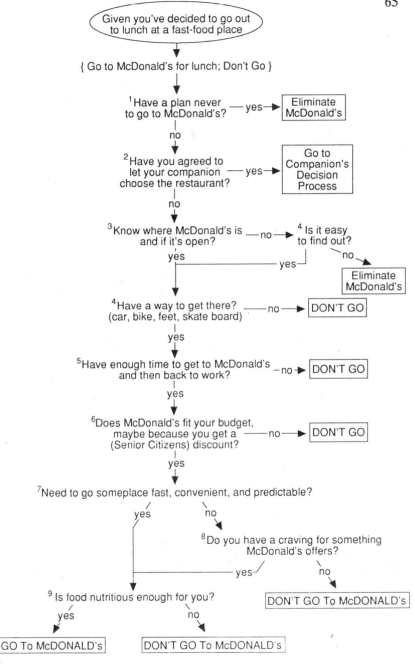

Figure 4.4 Alternative Model of Decision to Go to McDonald's

may be other criteria in this decision: we are not proposing this model as a final testable model of this decision but only as a first reworking of the vine in Figures 4.2–4.3.)

The third way to devine a tree is to identify and eliminate decision criteria that belong in a logically prior (or later) decision and put them in another tree. We discuss this strategy more in Chapter 5; here we should just mention that vines often occur instead of trees because the modeler has not yet realized that he or she has a *series* of trees to model, not just one, which means that the modeler has not yet identified decision criteria that belong in a logically prior (or later) decision tree and can be taken out of this tree. In the McDonald's decision model of Figure 4.2, criterion 1, "Do you ever have lunch out?" is the output of a logically-prior decision to go out for lunch somewhere, anywhere, which occurs logically, if not temporally, before the decision of where to go for lunch. It and criterion 2, "Always eat lunch at another place?" can be generalized to criterion 1 in the more concise tree in Figure 4.4, "Have a plan never to go to McDonald's?" This latter criterion can account for people who have rules (script rules, described in Chapter 5) to always eat fast foods, or never eat at McDonald's again because of a previous bad experience. Because script rules allow one to rapidly eliminate an alternative, we put this criterion in stage 1.

Common Problem #6: Another Outcome Suddenly Appears

Students often run into the problem that another outcome suddenly appears in the outcome boxes [   ] that was not present in the initial set of alternatives {   } at the top of the tree. For example, in the lunch at McDonald's decision in Figure 4.4, the outcome [Go to Burger King] may suddenly appear after a "no" answer to criterion 8, as in Figure 4.5. This new outcome is chosen by informant 10 in the model-building sample and the student, unthinking, pencils it into the model. But this is not logical: Each outcome at the end of a path must also be an option in the set of alternatives at the top of the tree. What does the student do — also pencil the new option in the set of alternatives at the top of the tree? Can we rewrite the set of alternatives at the top of the tree to be {Go to McDonald's; go to Burger King}?

That solution doesn't always work because the new set of alternatives implies that if an informant doesn't go to McDonald's, he or she does go to Burger King, and vice versa. Moreover, it changes the whole decision. It replaces the simple decision {Go to McDonald's; don't} with a broader, more complicated study of the decision between fast-food restaurants. As mentioned in step 2 in Chapter 2, this is a harder decision to study because there are more fast-food restaurants in most United States towns than McDonald's and Burger King; these two do not form an exhaustive set of alternatives. To properly model this

67

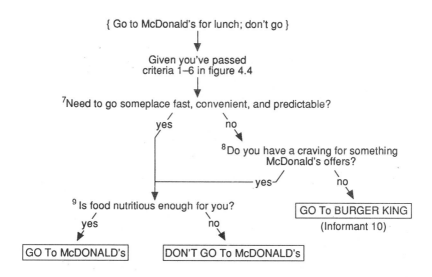

Figure 4.5 One Informant's Decision Model

broader decision, the student must interview people who go and don't go to *each* of these fast-food restaurants in town, and that takes more time than most students have.

The student has two acceptable solutions to this problem. First, he or she can stick with the original set of decision alternatives {Go to McDonald's; don't}, and change informant 10's outcome back to [Don't go to McDonald's], leaving unspecified the restaurant where he or she actually goes.

Another acceptable solution is to change the initial set of alternatives to {Go to McDonald's; go to fast-food restaurant X}, where fast-food restaurant X is the last fast-food place in town that the informant went to lunch. However, this change also necessitates a change in stage 2 of the decision model because now the informant must explicitly compare McDonald's to fast-food restaurant X instead of simply passing McDonald's through a set of criteria it must pass. The new stage 2 might look like Figure 4.6, in which criterion 7 is now an explicit ordering aspect which orders McDonald's and fast-food restaurant X on convenience and predictability. Now the decision maker goes to McDonald's only if it's more convenient and predictable than restaurant X or he or she has a craving for something McDonald's offers, and also passes nutrition constraint 9. (But what if the student ignores the existence of the ordering aspect? This problem is discussed next.)

68

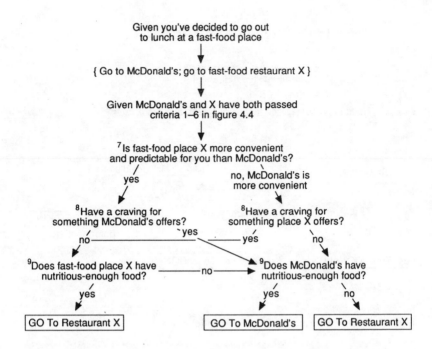

Figure 4.6 Stage 2 of the Revised Decision Model of Lunch at McDonald's

Note that a change in the model also means the questionnaire to test the model must now be changed, not only because stage 2 is changed but also because fast-food restaurant X in addition to McDonald's must now pass stage 1 constraints. In summary, the moral of this story is: every time there's a new outcome found, there's a change in the set of alternatives, a change in the model, and a change in the questionnaire. Most students don't want to get into all these changes, but decision makers are great at coming up with new unexpected choices.

Homework 4.1: Revise the questionnaire to test the new model of the lunch decision at McDonald's in Figure 4.6. Be sure you revise questions to test both stages 1 and 2.

Common Problem #7: There is No Ordering Aspect

In Figures 4.4 through 4.6, the ordering aspect that is "maximized" in this decision is "convenience and predictability of a fast-food place," criterion 7. This aspect signals the start of stage 2, the hard-core part of the decision process described in Chapter 5. But this aspect is often obscured in real-life decisions. It is especially hidden in simple {Go to

X, don't go} decisions or {Do Y; don't do Y} decisions in which the decision maker chooses between going to X and doing Y versus continuing with the status quo and not going to X or doing Y. In this simplest kind of decision, all aspects — even the ordering aspect — look like constraints which must be passed, e.g., [7]"Need to go someplace fast, convenient, and predictable?" If this need doesn't exist, the informant doesn't go to McDonald's. In reality, the decision maker is *comparing* the two alternatives (going to X (or McDonald's) versus not going) on some — at least one — aspect. If the alternative "Go to McDonald's" is not comparably better than the alternative "Don't go," the decision maker won't go or deviate from the status quo. In this regard, microeconomic theory is correct: *something —some aspect —is maximized or minimized in every choice, subject to constraints* (Henderson and Quandt, 1958).[13]

What happens to decision models when students *miss* the ordering aspect and don't have one in their models? Sometimes nothing: The ordering aspect is phrased like criterion 7 in terms of need so that it seems like a constraint, and the model predicts just fine. The model appears *as if* decision makers are *satisficing* because nothing is maximized. Other times, however, especially with more complicated models with more than one alternative, an ordering aspect like criterion 7 in Figure 4.6 is needed to route or send the alternatives in order down the tree and through the constraints. This routing of alternatives through constraints is what the ordering aspect does; this is its function. It gives "the edge" to one alternative over the others and tells the decision maker which alternative gets a crack at passing the set of constraints first, before the other alternatives. If the "best" alternative passes all the constraints, it is chosen. Only when the alternative ranked first on the ordering aspect *fails* a constraint do the other alternatives get a chance at passing them. In Figure 4.6, for example, if McDonald's is more convenient than fast-food place X and the decision maker has no special craving for something at restaurant X, then McDonald's gets first crack at passing the nutrition constraint 9 on the right-hand path of the tree. Otherwise, fast-food place X gets first crack at passing constraint 9, if the decision maker has no special craving for something at McDonald's. Without the ordering aspect in the model, the routing (or ordering of these alternatives through the constraints) is ad hoc at best. At worst, the model without an ordering aspect or with the wrong ordering aspect can be wrong, i.e., make an error by letting the wrong alternative through the constraints first to be incorrectly chosen by the model. There is thus always an ordering aspect; it's just that, in some models, the ordering aspect lies hidden and unrecognized. Don't worry, however: In the next chapter, as we let *The Thing* out, they'll also come out of the closet.

5. HOW TO BUILD MULTI-STAGE MODELS

This chapter describes how to build more complicated decision models, i.e., multi-alternative and multi-stage models and a series of sequential decision models. Described are how to model a multi-stage decision process and how to expand a decision model to include new subroutines and become a series of related decision models incorporating feedback loops. An example of a multi-stage model is the lunch at McDonald's decision; an example of a series of decision models is the woman professional's job search decision. Briefly, the methodological debates in the literature are summarized.

In Chapter 4, we worked on the decision model to go to McDonald's for lunch, until it became a multi-alternative, multi-stage model with both stage-1 criteria (1–6) and stage-2 criteria (7–9). It is shown in Figure 5.1 to illustrate some of the complexities that a realistic model of a real-life choice has, as compared to the simple {Do it, don't do it} decision models of Chapters 2 and 3. After modeling these simple kinds of decisions, we are now ready to move on to build more complicated decision models, which, like Figure 5.1, have some of these complexities.

The Theory Behind Decision Tree Models

There is a theory of choice behind decision tree models described in such detail elsewhere that we need not reproduce all of it here (Gladwin, 1976, 1977, 1980). However, the modeler should know what basic assumptions lie behind a multi-stage hierarchical model so that he or she does not confuse it with another model, such as a lexicographic ordering model, which is also hierarchical but has different assumptions. The theory behind a multi-stage tree model assumes that an alternative is a set of characteristics or aspects; an aspect is a dimension or feature of an alternative. Further, all aspects are discrete; when decision makers use a continuous quantitative dimension such as cost, they treat it as a constraint (e.g., is cost of car_1 < \$4000?) or they categorize it such that there is an ordering or a semiordering with noticeable differences of the alternatives on the aspect (cost of car_1 < cost of car_2). An algebraic form of decision model follows from this assumption.

The theory postulates that in choosing between a large number of objects, decision makers go through multiple stages during the decision process. In stage 1, they eliminate rapidly, often *preattentively* (Gladwin and Murtaugh, 1980), all alternatives that have some unwanted aspect; this is Tversky's (1972) elimination-by-aspects theory

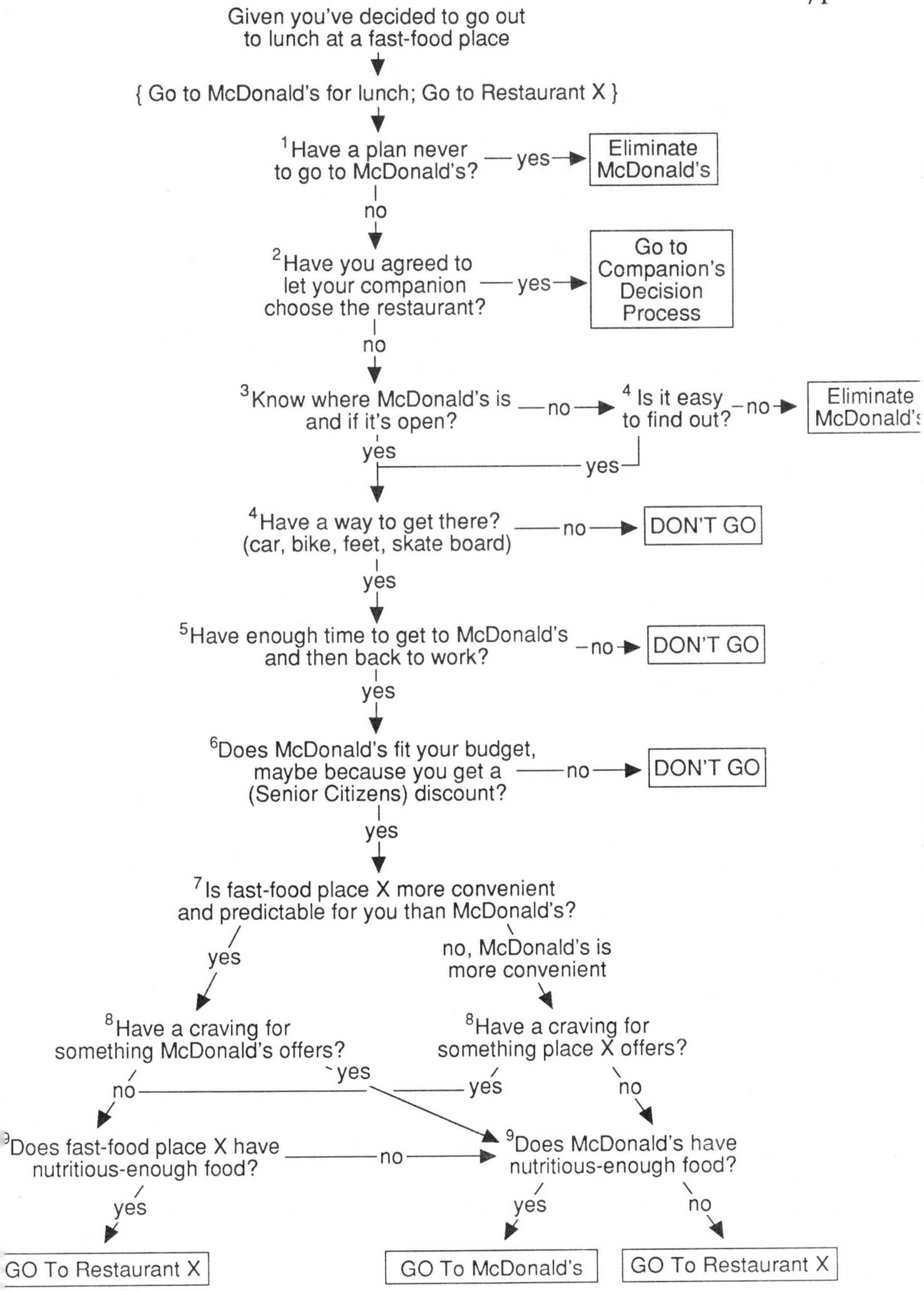

Figure 5.1 Revised Decision Model to Go to McDonald's for Lunch

of choice. In a choice between used cars, for example, a car buyer scans the used-car ads and eliminates all trucks, vans, convertibles, two-door sedans, and cars over eight years old and over $4000. After passing all alternatives through stage-one constraints, which are *not ordered* in importance — in contrast to a lexicographic ordering model in which stage-one criteria are ordered in importance — the decision maker is left with a small number of alternatives (two or four) to decide about in a more detailed way in stage 2.

People typically think the real decision process is the latter stage 2, in which the decision maker chooses among the two to four alternatives by first eliminating (or not even considering) aspects on which alternatives have equal or equivalent values. For example, if two alternative cars are both under $4000, the car buyer does not consider the constraint, "Is cost < $4000." Then the decision maker chooses an aspect on which to order the alternatives (e.g., comfort of car_1 > comfort of car_3), formulates or considers constraints on the alternatives, and passes the ordered alternatives through the constraints which, like stage-one constraints, are *not* ordered. If the alternative ordered first on the ordering aspect "comfort" does not satisfy all the constraints, the alternative ordered second on comfort gets a chance at them. If no alternative passes all the constraints, another strategy (e.g., further search) is employed. This "hard-core" choice process of stage 2 is essentially an algebraic version of "maximization subject to constraints," the basic choice principle of micro-economics. It is an algebraic version of that choice principle because there is an *ordering* of alternatives on an aspect rather than maximization of a continuous quantitative aspect, as in most micro-economics texts. The entire multi-stage model is thus a combination of Tversky's elimination-by-aspects theory (stage 1) and micro-economists' maximization-subject-to-constraints theory (stage 2). The algebraic form of the model results in a series of decision trees, tables, or sets of decision rules (Gladwin, 1975, 1980).

For practical purposes, this theory of choice is useful to keep in mind only with more complicated decisions, e.g., decisions with multiple alternatives and subroutines. As noted at the end of Chapter 4, in the simplest {Do it; don't do it} decision with one alternative to be accepted or rejected, one doesn't even notice the lack of an ordering aspect because it looks just like a constraint. However, when the decision model gets more complicated and multiple alternatives appear, the modeler needs to distinguish stage-one and stage-two constraints and needs an ordering aspect to order the alternatives through stage-two constraints. This point can best be understood by *doing* the following homework problem.[13]

Homework 5.1: Now, let's *broaden* the set of alternatives in the decision between fast-food luncheon restaurants to the set of: {all fast-food luncheon restaurants in town}, {all fast-food luncheon restaurants near the university}, or {McDonald's, Burger King, Archie's, or Kentucky Fried Chicken}. The class might take on this more realistic real-life decision as a class project and divide into three or more teams. Let the different teams interview decision makers in each of the different restaurants in the new set of alternatives. Limit the luncheon restaurants to fast-food places, because if we open up the set of alternatives to any luncheon place, slow or fast, *The Thing* will destroy us. Teams should answer the following questions. Question$_1$: What does the ordering aspect look like now? Question$_2$: Do decision makers *compare* all alternatives in the expanded set on at least one aspect, or do they eliminate two or three alternatives in stage 1 and then use a model similar to Figure 5.1 in stage 2? After each team models the decision to go to "its" restaurant, the class as a whole should look for similarities in the models developed by the different teams and put the different models together into one composite model.

Homework 5.2: Now develop the questionnaire to test this decision with the broader set of alternatives, and test the model that the class as a whole has come up with. Note that now questions testing criteria must be asked of *each* alternative in the beginning set of alternatives. So make some columns for each alternative, as in Table 5.1, and write the yes/no answers to the questions in the appropriate column. Remember the moral of Chapter 3: Every time we change the model, we change the questionnaire used to test the model.

Letting *The Thing* Out: Sequential Decision Trees

Now that you've seen the need for a multi-stage model and the usefulness of an ordering aspect, let's complicate your life still further. Let's talk about how to cope with decision models that suddenly start to expand—like *The Thing,* the being in the movie of the same name that clones itself at subzero temperatures and becomes more and more huge and complicated—from one tree to five or six, as we elicit unless conditions to the original unless conditions and exceptions to the exceptions to the rule (Harris, 1974). As an example, let's expand the model of the fast-food restaurant decision into a series of three recursive or time-sequential models in which the decision maker first decides to go out to lunch, then decides to go to lunch at a fast-food place rather than a slow, elegant, sit-down restaurant, and finally decides whether to eat lunch at McDonald's or fast-food place X. The phrase "Given you've decided to" in the circle preceding the set of alternatives at the top of the tree means that this decision is the second or third or n^{th} in a

74

Table 5.1 What Your Questionnaire to Test a Model with a Broader Set of Alternatives in Stage 1 Might Look Like

STAGE-ONE QUESTIONS:	McD's	B. King	Archie's	K. F. Chicken
1) Have a plan never to go to _____? (McD's, B.K., A's, K.F.C.)				
2) Have you agreed to let your luncheon companion choose the restaurant?				
3) Know where _____ is and if it's open? (McD's, B.K., A's, K.F.C.)				
4) Is it easy to find out where _____ is? (McD's, B.K., A's, K.F.C.)				
5) Have a way to get to _____? (McD's, B.K., A's, K.F.C.)				
6) Have enough time to get to _____ and then back to work? (McD's, B.K., A's, K.F.C.)				
7) Does _____ fit your budget, (McD's, B.K., A's, K.F.C.) maybe because you get a (Senior Citizens) discount?				

series of decisions that are either related logically or made at different times.[14] But what if you, the beginning modeler, have not written such a "Given that" phrase at the top of your tree? How do you realize you are studying a series of decisions rather than just one real-life decision? How do you go on to model a series of decisions? As in Chapters 2 and 3, you can follow a cognitive plan which has well-defined steps, now outlined.

STEP 1.

Recognize the signs that there is more than one decision to be modeled in the decision context you're studying. Fortunately, there are signals that the decision model you're working on is becoming a more complicated series of decision models, and *The Thing* is getting out.

One such sign is that the tree that should be beautiful instead becomes a tangly, never-ending vine, like the one in Figures 4.2 and 4.3 in Chapter 4. Vines occur instead of trees because the modeler has not yet realized that he or she has a series of trees to model, not just one.

Thus the modeler has not yet identified decision criteria that belong in a logically prior (or posterior) decision tree and has not yet put them in another tree. Note that criteria 1 in the vine of Figure 4.2, "Do you ever have lunch out?" is the output of a logically-prior decision to go out for lunch somewhere, anywhere, which logically occurs before the decision of *where* to go for lunch. Once we realize this to be the case, we can take criterion 1 out of the vine, put it on another piece of paper, and make a note to model that logically-prior decision in the near future.

Another clear signal that the decision model is becoming a series of models is the sudden appearance of an unexpected outcome, different from those in the set of alternatives at the top of the tree, in one of the outcome boxes. As noted in Chapter 4, to solve this problem, the modeler cannot simply change the initial set of alternatives at the top of the tree without changing the whole decision (and maybe adding an ordering aspect) and also changing the questionnaire to test the model. Rather than making all these changes in the initial model, the modeler should ask if the new, unexpected outcome belongs in a related decision that feeds into the initial decision model.

A third sign is the appearance of a criterion or constraint that doesn't seem to make any sense or belong to the alternatives in this decision. In this case, the criterion might belong in another related decision. For example, in Figure 4.2, criterion 7, "Want to play one of the games?" and criterion 8, "Want a Happy Meal," do not quite belong in an adult's luncheon decision. This is thus a sign that there is another related decision, the child's decision of where to go for lunch, which is linked to (and feeds into) the adult's decision via criterion 2, "Have you agreed to let your luncheon companion choose the restaurant," in Figure 5.1.

A fourth signal is that the tree you're drawing goes off the piece of paper, and the decision rule or table you're putting together gets too long and complicated. These are symptoms, of course. The underlying illness is that the decision model has started to expand from one tree to three or four, and you need to add a subroutine or two to your computer program because you have gotten into the complexities of real-life decision making.

The beginning modeler should therefore examine the shape of the tree, and the outcomes that end up in the outcome boxes after interviews with more informants, and even the elicited criteria and ask: "Is this a vine instead of a tree? After the last interview, has a new, unexpected outcome appeared in the tree? Have informants come up with criteria that don't seem to fit in this decision, or has the string of unless conditions gotten too complicated? Could this criterion and that outcome belong in another decision related to but different from the decision now being modeled? If the answer to any of these questions is "yes," continue on to step 2.

STEP 2.

Identify the other related decisions in the series, and figure out which decisions are logically prior to which. For practical purposes, it is irrelevant whether the decisions in the series are made recursively (i.e., at different points of time) or simultaneously but such that one decision follows logically from another decision or feeds into another decision. With regard to the lunch at McDonald's decision, we can identify three sequential decisions:

    (1) the decision, made at time t, to go out to lunch versus eat in the office versus eat at home

    (2) the decision, made at time t+1, to go to lunch at a fast-food place rather than a slow, elegant, sit-down restaurant

    (3) the decision, made at time t+2, of whether to eat lunch at McDonald's or fast-food place X (Figure 5.1)

Again, times t, t+1, and t+2 can be seconds apart; we really don't care how recursively or simultaneously these decisions are made. The aim is just to simplify the decision problem so that it can be modeled in a logical way and the trees (or tables) can be contained on one piece of paper or computer screen.

STEP 3.

Once the sequence of decisions is specified, model each decision by following the steps outlined in chapters 2 and 3, i.e., interview more informants, identify the alternatives and criteria in each decision, and make up a composite model(s) to test. In the series of decisions leading to lunch at McDonald's, the first two decisions can be modeled and tested, just as the logically-later decision to go to McDonald's was modeled and tested using the methodological steps described in Chapters 2 and 3. The models will be multi-alternative models, probably multi-stage models, and similar to Figure 5.1.

An Example: The Woman Professional's Job Shift Decision

A good example of a series of related decisions, rather than just one decision, is provided by the woman Ph.D.'s job shift decision. The model in Figures 5.2–5.6 was developed because women academics receive lower salary and rank than men, are less likely to be tenured, and advance more slowly up the academic ladder. Why is this so if the barriers to parallel advancement of men and women are falling (Lane, 1981)? One explanation, advanced by Rosenfeld (1981) to explain slower transition rates of women between academic ranks is that:

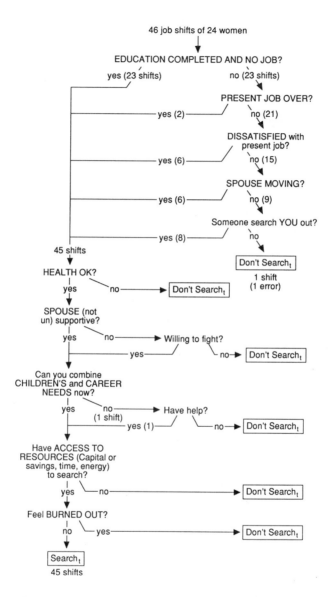

Figure 5.2 The Woman Professional's Decision to Search for a New Job at Time$_t$

(1) academia is essentially a national market in specialized positions, (2) upward mobility in academia requires strategic *job shifts* and geographic moves, and (3) taking advantage of strategic moves is easier for

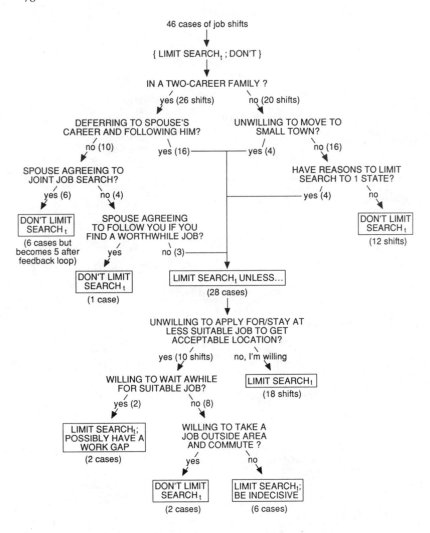

Figure 5.3 Woman Professional's Decision to Limit or Not Limit Search to Small Geographical Region at Time$_t$, Given a Search$_t$

men than women because of marriage hypergamy, the tendency of women to marry men of equal or higher status than their own. Thus, women rather than men professionals are more likely to be in two-career families, which adversely affect their career development because they are then more likely to be limited by *geographic immobility*. In contrast, few men academics are in two-career families and thus limited to geographic immobility.

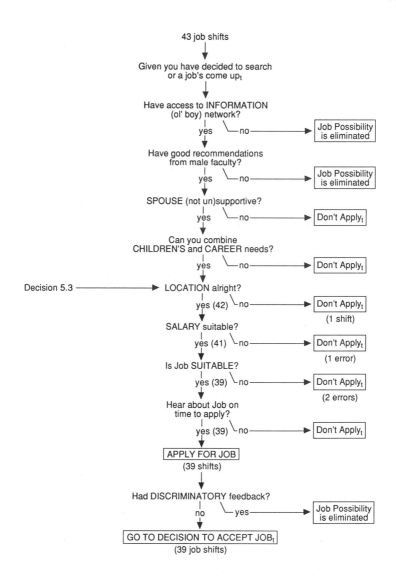

Figure 5.4 Decision to Apply for Job I at Time $_{t+1}$

In the decision models developed and tested via telephone interviews with half the population of women agricultural economists in the United States (Gladwin, 1982b), the unit of analysis is the woman's *job shift* between institutions or positions within an institution. The methodology assumes that each job shift requires the individual woman to make

80

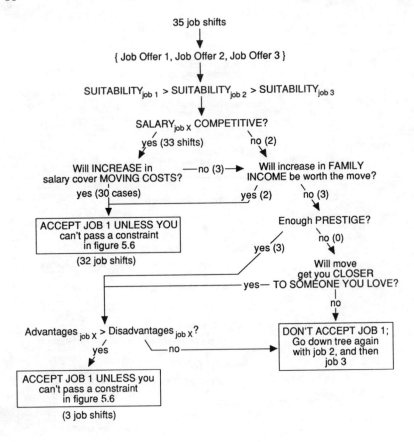

Figure 5.5 Decision to Accept a Job

one or more job-search decisions. By modeling these decisions, a researcher should be able to identify geographical immobility as a factor limiting job search and job acceptance, if, in fact, it is a factor. Testing this model were data on 46 job shifts made by 24 women. The series of models assumes that the woman makes four interrelated sequential decisions:

(1) the decision to *search for a job* in agricultural economics at time t (Figure 5.2)

(2) the decision to *limit the search* (or not to limit it) to a smaller geographical region than the United States at time t (Figure 5.3)

(3) the decision to *apply for a job* at time t+1, given search at time t (Figure 5.4)

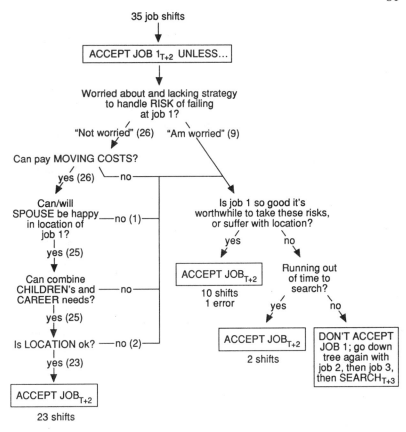

Figure 5.6 Constraints on Decision to Accept a Job Offer

(4) the decision to *accept a job* at time t+2, given (an) offer(s) (Figures 5.5 and 5.6)

Once the time-sequence of decisions made by women Ph.D.s was determined (step 2), I identified the decision criteria in each tree model (step 3). In Figure 5.2, these include reasons to search, at the top of the tree: the woman has completed her Ph.D. and/or has no job offer now, she's dissatisfied with present job, her spouse is moving, or someone has searched her out. Given a reason, she still does not search if she cannot pass constraints of good health, a supportive or at least not *un*supportive spouse, and capital and time to search. If she has children, she must feel that she can satisfy her children's and career needs at the same time and not feel so burned out by career demands that she considers changing careers altogether. In Figure 5.3, the decision to limit or not limit the search, made prior to the decision to apply for a specific job, the first criterion is a woman's presence in a two-career family with spouse not perfectly mobile. Single women and older women with retired or easily-movable spouses (with 20 job shifts) go down the right-hand side of the tree, mostly to the "Don't limit search" outcome; while women in two-career families (with 26 job shifts) go down the left-hand side of the tree, mostly to the "Limit search" outcome. Of these latter cases, the woman receives a joint job offer in only three cases, and the spouse agrees to follow the woman in only two cases. These data thus support the hypothesis that the tendency for married women to be in two-career marriages also results in geographic immobility for women. Twenty-eight cases proceed down the path "Limit search unless. . . ." Women are asked if they are willing or unwilling to apply for a "less-suitable" job (defined as one with less salary or rank, more dissatisfaction, and/or less compatibility with lifetime goals than the women are qualified for) in order to get an acceptable geographical location. In this sample, 18 women are willing and thus choose to Limit search; 10 women are unwilling to apply for (stay at) a less-suitable job than they qualify for.

Note that the output of the "Limit search" decision feeds into the "Location alright?" criterion in Figure 5.4, the woman's decision to apply for a specific job; 43 cases of job shifts make it to this decision point, and 39 cases reach the outcome, "Apply for job." In Figures 5.5 and 5.6, the woman decides to accept or reject a specific job offer(s). If the time between job offers is large enough, the woman may process one job offer at a time without comparing alternative offers. In this case, the ordering aspect appears like a constraint, e.g., "Is job suitable?" In this sample of 43 job-shift cases (Figure 5.4), 19 women had multiple offers to choose between, and 24 women had single offers to accept or reject. In Figure 5.5 are the reasons for a woman to accept a job offer; these include criteria of suitability of the job to long-run career interests, salary, family income, prestige, and "closeness of the job to someone you love." Any of these criteria may be the ordering aspect; to allow for more individual variation in this model, I asked women to choose their ordering aspect by asking, "What's more important to you, suitability of the job, salary, prestige, etc." In 35 cases, suitability is "maximized" and is the ordering aspect: these cases are reported in Figures 5.5 and 5.6.[15] In Figure 5.6 are the constraints to acceptance of the job at time t+2; 23 of 35 cases pass all constraints of risk (of the woman's not being able to handle the job), capital to pay moving costs, spouse's and children's happiness, and again, location. In 10 cases of job shifts, the woman considers the job risky but so good that it's worthwhile to take the risks; while in two cases, there is no other job offer and no more time to search, so she takes the job.

STEP 4.

Once all decisions are modeled, check them for logical consistency and the proper "fit" of the decision criteria. Ask yourself: Do the criteria fit in the decision model they're in now; do they belong to that decision? Note that some criteria are in every decision model in the series because the decision maker asks these questions at every step in the decision process. For example, the "Location alright?" criterion is in both Figures 5.4 and 5.6; the "Job suitable?" criterion is in Figures 5.3, 5.4, and 5.5; and the "Can you combine children's and career needs?" criterion is in Figures 5.2, 5.4, and 5.6. There may also be a subtle change in other decision criteria: e.g., the criterion "Spouse (*not un*) supportive?" occurs in Figures 5.2 and 5.4, the decisions to search and apply for a new job. This criterion changes subtly to a more demanding criterion, "Can/will spouse be *happy* in the location of the job?" as the job candidate has to decide whether to really accept the job (Figure 5.6). This subtle difference in the job candidate's attitude toward the spouse's happiness makes good sense if the candidate wants to stay married.

STEP 5.

Add feedback loops in models where they belong to allow decision makers to go back and forth between the related decisions. This allows more flexibility and simultaneity between the models (Simon, personal communication). In the woman's job shift decision series, for example, there are two feedback loops shown in Figure 5.7. The first feedback loop starts from the outcome [Limit search$_t$] in Figure 5.3, and, at time $t+1$, asks the decision maker if a "suitable" job came up. If it did, the woman is sent on to Figure 5.4 to apply for the job; if not, it asks if a "less-suitable" job came up. If it did, again the woman is sent to apply for the job. If not again, she is sent or fed back to START in Figure 5.2 to renew the search-decision process. The second feedback loop allows the woman to go from the decision to limit the search (Figure 5.3) to the decision to apply for a job (Figure 5.4), then to the decision to accept the job (Figures 5.5 and 5.6), and then back to the decision (*not*) to limit the search (Figure 5.3) this time, after she decided not to accept a job. Clearly, feedback loops help the series of decision models to be more realistic choice models by allowing the decision makers to be more spontaneous, appear indecisive, and search further.

Homework 5.3: To practice modeling a series of decisions, model the two decisions made (logically) prior to Figure 5.1, the decision to go to

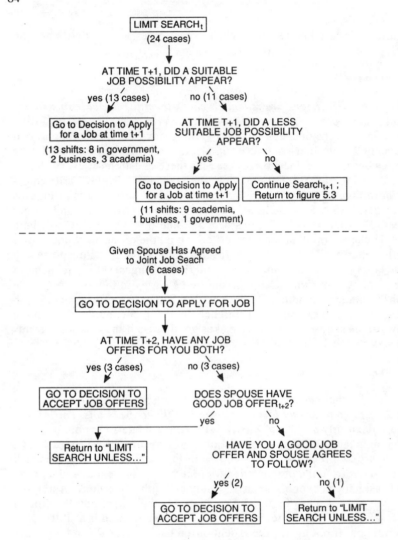

Figure 5.7 Feedback Loops Between the Decisions

lunch at a fast-food restaurant. Do it individually, instead of as a class project, in order to practice juggling a series of decision models instead of just one. Then put the decision trees you've developed side by side and be sure the criteria fit in each decision model. Check to see if the models are complementary to each other and fit together logically and sequentially. Put in feedback loops where appropriate.

Further Complexities

The purpose of this monograph has been to describe how to do ethnographic decision tree modeling. To accomplish this goal in 96 pages, I have skipped over many of the methodological debates in the literature. This is not to say that the debates are trivial or tepid. To date, there are three classes of debates. First, Chibnick (1980) claims that it is not necessary to posit cognitive rule-based models of the decision process; instead one should use a "statistical-behavior approach" based on standard statistical tests to study decision makers' behavior.[16] Second, decisions made routinely become *preattentive* plans or scripts (H. Gladwin and Murtaugh, 1980; Schank and Abelson, 1977). Third, there is so much individual variation in decision rules, goals, and roles that group decision models are inadequate and unrealistic cognitive models (Quinn, 1978; Gardner, 1985).

We close this chapter by summarizing the counterarguments to the above arguments. Quinn (1975: 28) counters Chibnick's (1980) argument that it is not necessary to posit cognitive rule-based models of the decision process; she claims that decision models that ignore cognition are like "machines with their insides missing." Mukhopadhyay (1984) notes, however, that the standard statistical tests advocated by Chibnick and perfected in probit and logit analysis can be used to *indirectly* test a rule-based model. Cognitive rule-based models of the decision process can be used to generate hypotheses about behavior resulting from the decisions made; then standard statistical tests can be used to test those hypotheses. Unfortunately, they can provide this test for only a few of the variables or criteria in an individual's decision process. Because real-life decision models become very large and complicated with a great number of variables/criteria processed, as we have seen in this chapter, decision models should be tested directly, as done here.

I agree with the second argument that decisions made routinely become *preattentive* plans or scripts, like scripts in a play (Gladwin and Murtaugh, 1980; Schank and Abelson, 1977). A script is a sequence of rules which tell the actors who does what, when, and for how long, or how to do X. Throughout this monograph, for example, you have been attentively following my "expert-systems" script of how to build and test decision models. To the outsider, the rules in Chapters 2, 3, and 5 could be considered to be a set of decision rules; to the insider like myself, however, they are not decision rules because I am not aware of having made a decision. The decision is made so frequently that the rules become part of a script. I usually follow this script preattentively, but have purposefully brought it to an attentive level for didactic purposes. In time, your own rules for building tree models will become routinized into a script; hopefully it will diffuse to your students.

Scripts are sets of routinized decision rules; nevertheless, I would qualify Schank and Abelson's (1977: 43) scripts to include embedded decision points. They include, for example, the decision of what to eat as a step in their restaurant script ("S MBUILDs choice of F"), but there is no model of how that decision is made. Decisions can be considered "entry conditions" to a script, but, in that case, any step in a plan or script sequence can be a complicated decision subroutine, modeled by a decision tree (Gladwin and Butler, 1984: 211). Following Werner and Schoepfle (1987) who allow for subplans embedded in plans and model the choice between alternative subplans, we can complicate the picture of a plan or script by embedding decision subroutines in the plan. In rule form, these are the "exceptions to the exceptions to the rule" noted by Harris (1974). Thus decision models and scripts are both necessary to model real-life decision behavior: they are complementary models.

Countering the third argument proposing only individual decision process models (Quinn, 1978; Gardner, 1985) is the fact that *policy planners have to make policy for groups of people* and not individuals. The elicitation of one individual's "expert systems" may be cognitively interesting, but for applied purposes, it is of limited usefulness except for teaching purposes, as this monograph attempts. Of much greater use to policymakers, as is shown in the next chapter, is the generalization of many individuals' decision criteria (usually emic) into a model for the group, which may be "eticized." Nevertheless, the fact that group decision models predict (and predict well, in some cases over 90% of) the decisions made by individuals in the group shows that *these generalizations work* pretty well. They work because individuals in the same culture do share knowledge systems and at least some, if not all, of their decision criteria.

6. WHAT'S THE PAYOFF?

Of what use are decision models? In Chapter 1, I listed a number of real-world problems: The increase in use of hard drugs by teenagers, the decrease in the number of Black college students, non-adoption of new biotechnologies by Third World farmers, the depletion of forests and marine fisheries, and the rise of teenage pregnancies. I claimed that the goal of decision studies was to model how people make real-world decisions and to identify the specific decision criteria used by most of the individuals in a group in order that policymakers might intervene in the decision-making process with new policies designed to make things better for the targeted group. How can policy recommendations be taken from a decision tree model? To answer this question, let's return to the model of the Malawi farmer's credit decision and formulate policy recommendations from the model. Keep in mind that the policy goal is to open up the credit institutions so that Malawi's farmers can get more credit in the future, use more fertilizer, and produce more maize to feed either their own families or the growing cities.

The model tested in Chapter 3 shows government policy planners why 21 farmers got credit for fertilizer in 1986/87, while 18 farmers did *not* get credit: seven farmers were excluded from farmers' clubs in their village, four farmers' clubs had defaulted and so were denied credit in 1986/87; three (women) farmers were too fearful of not repaying, and two (women) farmers were too hopelessly poor to even try to get into a club. These farmers eliminate the credit option rapidly, in the first stage of the decision process. Only 23 farmers pass to the "hard-core" decision process, where they compare the two options — getting credit versus buying fertilizer — on two aspects, cost and riskiness. In this stage, 19 farmers pass all constraints listed in the model and get at least some credit for fertilizer. Two more farmers, big farmers, felt that buying fertilizer was cheaper than getting credit but had other pressing needs for their cash. These farmers felt no risk of hunger because they had enough land to plant enough maize for family consumption but they feared not repaying the credit and so bought fertilizer. Two women remain as errors of the model because they get credit when, according to the model, they should buy fertilizer.

Given these results, researchers can make policy recommendations. This can be done, although the sample was admittedly small, because the model was tested and shown to predict between 85% (model 1) and 95% (model 2) of the historical choices made by a representative sample of the group or target audience. The specific policy recommendations made in this case are that government should continue to encourage expansion of clubs and eliminate some of the local club restrictions which exclude farmers. They should develop new terms of repayment which do not scare off farmers, especially women, from getting credit. One way this can be done is for government to subsidize each club's "credit fund," which is used to give amortized disaster loans to individual members when they default. These policies will probably not, however, reach the smallest of the smallholders, including many women household heads. Only a grant of supervised fertilizer for a couple of years will be sufficient to shock the smallest of the smallholders out of their "hopeless" constraint. Once they are shocked out of this constraint, they may proceed to minimize cost, as do their more hopeful neighbors.

Even though these policy recommendations are made about a mundane, earthy topic like fertilizer, similar policy results can be drawn from a similar study of any real-life choice people make. For example, previous results helped agronomists and planners of a rural development project to drop an agronomic recommendation that was impeding spread of new technology (Gladwin, 1976, 1979a, 1979b). In a similar vein, results from a model of Omaha, Nebraska teenagers' decisions about sex and birth control — decisions which lead to early pregnancies — are helping educators learn how and where to intervene in the process and with what information (Langworthy, personal communication). Similar models of teenagers' choice of drugs could help psychologists and social workers identify the main reasons teenagers switch from soft to hard drugs; while results from a model of Blacks' college enrollment could help educators identify the main reasons their enrollment is down in the 1980s. Results from a political scientist's study of congressional voting choices could help consumer advocacy groups lobby Congress; while those from a model to go to McDonald's for lunch could help McDonald's market researchers to capture more of the lunchtime market, and so on.

Helping policy planners make critically important policy decisions is only one of three ways ethnographic decision tree modeling can be useful. Testable models of real-world decision processes also provide social scientists with feedback about their behavioral theories. These models say whether the economic, sociological, educational, or psychological behavior studied conforms to a priori assumptions and accepted theories or whether something else — something completely unexpected — is going on and explaining most of the observed decision behavior.

Finally, decision tree models can also provide valuable feedback to social planners about why an applied project (a rural development project, public health, or educational project) aimed at helping some target clientele group do something is *failing*. Experience with such projects in Third World settings shows that the most frequent reason they fail is that they end up getting a very good answer to the *wrong* question. In Peru, for example, agronomists at the International Potato Center (CIP) designed a new, more efficient storage shed for potatoes that farmers did not adopt because, traditionally, they store potatoes inside, not outside, their homes (Rhoades, Booth, Shaw, and Werge, 1982). In Mexico, planners of the Puebla Project designed fertilizer demonstrations so that farmers would fertilize at planting and increase their yields; most farmers did not adopt because, with "the traditional way," they applied fertilizer before the rains came anyway, so the new technology would not increase their yields (Gladwin, 1979a).

In each case in which the development project failed, social scientists were involved in the project at the design stage as they should be (Matlon, Cantrell, King, and Benoit-Cattin, 1984), gathering lots of good quantitative data. In the case of the Plan Puebla, for example, good socioeconomic "baseline data" were collected, as well as data about centimeters of rainfall, soil types, and communication networks (CIMMYT, 1971). Still farmers did not adopt. What was missing? At the start of the project, social scientists did not find out *why* the farmers do what they traditionally do. They did not identify farmers' cognitive strategies and the decision criteria behind "the traditional way" before they tried to improve on it (Gladwin, 1979a). They did not know the farmers' problems before they designed the solution, so they ended up getting a good answer to the wrong question; no one adopted, and the project failed.

A modeling of the decision processes underpinning the traditions of the target clientele can stop these failures of applied projects. If project designers understand the decision criteria and logic used by the target population, they can find the answers to the *right* questions. Clearly, the applicability of decision tree methodology is limited only by the imagination of you, the social scientist — and the space in your backpack as you travel by canoe down the Amazon, or hike into Timbuctoo, or venture into the local middle school to study teenagers' drug decisions. It has been my aim to give you a useful tool; it is my hope that this small monograph will find its way into your backpack. Pleasant journey!

NOTES

1. The reader should by now guess what my favorite bumper sticker is: "I Speak Farming." Most of my own decision research deals with crops, fertilizer, farm crises, and the juggling of farmwork and nonfarm work by farm women and men. The method illustrated with these examples, however, is applicable to any real-life choice the student wants to study.

2. In Chapter 2, I do not recommend such a small model-building sample (of nine informants); nor do I usually use such a small sample. In Chapter 3, we shall see the errors that occurred from relying on such a small sample. So why am I using this decision model as an example of the method? For didactic purposes, a model which has problems is of more value to the student than a model with fewer flaws, e.g., the Guatemalan cropping decision model.

3. This decision was taken from a Northwestern University freshman paper by Karen Rain, "A Decision Study to (Not) Buy a Breakfast Contract," 1979, paper prepared for Anthropology A01. Names of student informants are fictitious.

4. Please forgive me for nagging you to "work through" the decision trees in this book like math problems or puzzles to be solved. One cannot just read this text as one reads other social science texts. This method can only be learned by doing it as you go along in the manual. Hence the homework problems.

5. This occurred because I was in Malawi only seven weeks total. Ordinarily, I would not attempt a decision model study in only seven weeks. But in 1973-74, I had modeled farmers' credit-for-fertilizer decisions in Puebla, Mexico, and I knew some of the decision criteria to look for when interviewing farmers in Malawi. In spite of this previous study, however, only four decision criteria ended up to be identical in both the Mexico and Malawi models.

6. A total of 40 farmers were in both samples. Of these, 26 farmers were credit club members, and 14 were not; 22 farmers got credit for fertilizer in 1986/87, while 18 did not. Seventeen farmers were women household heads, three were couples interviewed together, and 20 were male household heads. Unhappily, credit questions were forgotten with one farmer. All questions to farmers were translated from English into Chichewa, either by government extension specialists familiar with the area or a trained assistant I hired on the weekends.

7. Because I am a single woman and a household head, I was chagrined to find that my model predicted choices of male household heads, but not those of female household heads! As this chapter goes on to demonstrate, I had to discover a new "hopeless" criterion I had omitted from the model and would never have thought of because I am rich enough to afford a fertilizer loan, and the Mexican farmers I had previously studied were also rich enough. Once again, I discovered my own ethnocentrism.

8. I discovered this criterion when I was looking for a very poor informant to interview, and so asked a woman with an obviously-malnourished baby on her back. The whole village ended up sitting with us around her little house, while she told me her

daughter had just left to get married, her husband had just deserted her, and she had no maize left, and she was too poor to join a credit club. All the time, she was breastfeeding the baby from a seemingly-empty breast. I felt terrible but kept asking my pre-ordained questions from my stilted questionnaire. Finally in desperation, a woman in the group said in a loud voice, "Look, what she's telling you is that *no-one* will give her credit in this village because she's just too poor."

9. Some of my students counter that they don't like to probe further, or push people around mentally. My counter-argument is: This is why one shouldn't use friends as informants. Modeling a decision is a little like solving a murder. To solve the murder, you will have to probe — politely, of course — and check up on people and be as unpopular as a detective.

10. For modeling purposes, it helps to think of decision trees as analogues of multiple-regression equations. The independent variables in a regression are decision criteria in the tree and the dependent variable in a regression is an outcome in the tree. Therefore, the decision criteria should be measured independently of the decision outcomes, just like the independent variables in a regression are measured independently of the dependent variable, in order to predict the dependent variable.

11. Sometimes in science, we learn more from negative results than positive results, e.g., the Michaelson-Morley experiment which tried to measure the velocity of light through "ether." Before the Michaelson-Morley experiment, everyone believed that light travels through ether, just as sound travels through air. So, two physicists set up apparatus on two mountains to measure the speed of light in two directions, hoping to find a difference in the two speeds due to the friction of ether in one direction. Unfortunately, they failed to find any significant effect of ether on the velocity of light. They were chagrined but didn't hide their results. Now, no one believes that light travels through ether. This should be your attitude: If your model predicts poorly, you've learned something from those negative results. Report them.

12. Micro-economists are not correct, however, in assuming that *utility or expected utility* is what is maximized in consumer choice. Postulating utility or satisfaction to be the ordering aspect is just an admission by researchers that they don't know what aspect is being maximized. In this regard, utility is like "ether," an outdated, empty notion; but, unlike ether, it is impossible to test and disprove its existence.

13. Again, we can best learn about trees by doing them.

14. There are debates about whether decisions in a series are made recursively (i.e., at different points of time) or simultaneously but such that one decision follows logically from another decision, or one decision takes logical precedence over another decision. These debates are related to the question of whether there is parallel or sequential processing in the brain. We don't want to get into that debate, which is unnecessary for our practical purposes. Here we will assume decisions are sequential, without stipulating whether they are time-sequential or logic-sequential.

15. In five more cases, "closeness to someone you love" is the ordering aspect, while in two cases "prestige of the job" is maximized, and in one case "salary" is maximized. In all, 43 job shifts test the model: 39 cases from the outcome "Apply for the job" in Figure 5.4, plus three errors of Figure 5.4, plus one woman who went down Figures 5.5 and 5.6 twice because she rejected the first job offer and accepted the second job offer.

16. Due to inadequate space, we refer the reader to the literature for a fuller understanding of the debates and the objections to decision tree models outlined so briefly here.

REFERENCES

Anderson, J. (1979). Perspective on models of uncertain decisions, in J. Roumasset, J. Boussard, & I. Singh (Eds.), *Risk, Uncertainty, and Agricultural Development.* (pp. 39-62). New York: Agricultural Development Council.

Anderson, J. R., Dillon, J. L., & Hardaker, J. B. (1977). *Agricultural Decision Analysis.* Ames: Iowa State University Press.

Arrow, K. J. (1951). The nature of preference and choice. *Social Choice and Individual Values.* New York: John Wiley.

Barlett, P. (1977). The structure of decision making in Paso. *American Ethnologist 4*(2), 285-307.

Benito, C. A. (1976). Peasants' response to modernization projects in *Minifundia Economies. American Journal of Agricultural Economics 58*(2), 143-151.

Cancian, F. (1972). *Change and Uncertainty in a Peasant Economy.* Stanford, CA: Stanford University Press.

Chibnick, M. (1980). Working out or working in: The choice between wage labor and cash cropping in rural Belize. *American Ethnologist 7*(1), 86-105.

CIMMYT (International Center for the Improvement of Maize and Wheat) (1971). *The Puebla Project 1967-69.* Mexico, D.F., Mexico: CIMMYT.

Dixon, R. (1982). Women in agriculture: Counting the labor force in developing countries. *Population and Development Review 8*(3), 539-566.

Gardner, H. (1985). *The Mind's New Science.* New York: Basic Books.

Gladwin, C. (1975). A model of the supply of smoked fish from Cape Coast to Kumasi. In S. Plattner (Ed.), *Formal Methods in Economic Anthropology* No. 4, pp. 77-127. Washington, D.C.: A Special Publication of the American Anthropological Association.

Gladwin, C. (1976). A view of the Plan Puebla: An application of hierarchical decision models. *American Journal of Agricultural Economics 58*(5), 881-87.

Gladwin, C. (1977). *A model of farmers' decisions to adopt the recommendations of Plan Puebla.* Unpublished doctoral dissertation, Stanford University.

Gladwin, C. (1979a). Cognitive strategies and adoption decisions: A case study of nonadoption of an agronomic recommendation. *Economic Development and Cultural Change 28*(1), 155-173.

Gladwin, C. (1979b). Production functions and decision models: Complementary models. *American Ethnologist 6*(4), 653-674.

Gladwin, C. (1980). A theory of real-life choice: Applications to agricultural decisions. In P. Barlett (Ed.), *Agricultural Decision Making: Anthropological Contributions to Rural Development* (pp. 45-85). New York: Academic Press.

Gladwin, C. (1982a). The role of a cognitive anthropologist in a farming systems program which has everything. *The Role of Anthropologists and Other Social Scientists in Interdisciplinary Teams Developing Improved Food Production Technology.* Los Banos, Laguna, The Philippines: The International Rice Research Institute.

93

Gladwin, C. (1982b). Job search decisions of women agricultural economists: Are they limited by geographical immobility? In S. Lane (Ed.), *Opportunities for Women in Agricultural Economics*, Proceedings of a symposium at the American Agricultural Economics Association meetings, Logan, Utah, Aug. 1-4.

Gladwin, C. (1983). Contributions of decision-tree methodology to a farming systems program. *Human Organization 42*(2), 146-157.

Gladwin, C. (1989). On the division of labor between economics and economic anthropology. In S. Plattner (Ed.), *Economic Anthropology*. Stanford, CA: Stanford University Press.

Gladwin, C., & Butler, J. (1984). Is gardening an adaptive strategy for Florida family farmers? *Human Organization 43*(3), 208-216.

Gladwin, C., & Zabawa, R. (1984). Microdynamics of contraction decisions: A cognitive approach to structural change. *American Journal of Agricultural Economics 6*(5), 829-835.

Gladwin, C., & Zabawa, R. (1986). After structural change: Are part-time or full-time farmers better off? In J. Molnar (Ed.), *Agricultural Change: Consequences for Southern Farms and Rural Communities* (pp. 39-60). Boulder (CO): Westview Press.

Gladwin, C., & Zabawa, R. (1987). Transformations of full-time farms in the U.S.: Can they survive? In M. Maclachlan (Ed.), *Household Economies and Their Transformations*. Philadelphia, PA: University Press of America.

Gladwin, H. (1971). Decision making in the Cape Coast (Fante) fishing and fish marketing system. Unpublished doctoral dissertation, Stanford University.

Gladwin, H., & Murtaugh, M. (1980). The attentive/pre-attentive distinction in agricultural decisions. In P. Barlett (Ed.), *Agricultural Decision Making* (pp. 115-136). New York: Academic Press.

Gladwin, H., & Murtaugh, M. (1984). Test of a hierarchical model of auto choice on data from the National Transportation Survey. *Human Organization 43*(3), 217-226.

Harris, M. (1974). Why a perfect knowledge of all the rules one must know to act like a native cannot lead to knowledge of how the natives act. *Journal of Anthropological Research 30*(4), 242-251.

Harris, M. (1979). *Cultural Materialism: The Struggle for a Science of Culture*. New York: Random House.

Hildebrand, P. (1981). Combining disciplines in rapid appraisal: The *sondeo* approach. *Agricultural Administration 8*, 423-432.

Kahneman, D., & Tversky, A. (1972). Subjective probability: a judgment of representativeness. *Cognitive Psychology 3*, 430-454.

Kahneman, D., & Tversky, A. (1982). The psychology of preferences. *Scientific American 246*, 160-173.

Kydd, J., & Christiansen, R. (1982). Structural change in Malawi since independence: Consequences of a development strategy based on large-scale agriculture. *World Development 10*(5), 355-375.

Lancaster, K. (1966). A new approach to consumer theory. *Journal of Political Economy 74*, 132-157.

Lane, S. (1981). Evidence on barriers to the parallel advancement of male and female agricultural economists. *American Journal of Agricultural Economics 63*(5), 1025-1031.

Lave, C., & March, J. (1975). *An Introduction to Models in the Social Sciences*. New York: Harper and Row.

94

Luce, R. D. (1956). Semi-orders and a theory of utility discrimination. *Econometrica 24*, 178-191.

Malinowski, B. (1922). *Argonants of the Western Pacific*. London, U.K.: Routledge and Kegan Paul, Ltd.

Matlon, P., Cantrell, R., David King, R., & Benoit-Cattin, M. (1984). *Coming Full Circle: Farmers' Participation in the Development of Technology*. Ottawa, Canada: International Development Research Centre.

Moscardi, E., & DeJanvry, A. (1977). Attitudes toward risk among peasants: An econometric approach. *American Journal of Agricultural Economics 59*(4), 710-716.

Mukhopadhyay, C. (1984). Testing a decision process model of the sexual division of labor in the family. *Human Organization 43*(3), 227-242.

Murtaugh, M., & Gladwin, H. (1980). A hierarchical decision-process model for forecasting automobile type choice. *Transportation Research 14A*, 337-348.

Pike, K. (1954). *Language in Relation to a Unified Theory of the Structure of Human Behavior*. The Hague: Mouton.

Quinn, N. (1971, Nov. 22-25). Simplifying procedures in natural decision-making. Paper presented at the Mathematical Social Science Board Seminar in Natural Decision Making Behavior, Palo Alto, California.

Quinn, N. (1975). Decision-making models of social structure. *American Ethnologist 2*, 19-46.

Quinn, N. (1978). Do Mfantse fish sellers estimate probabilities in their heads? *American Ethnologist 5*(2), 206-226.

Raiffa, H. (1968). *Decision Analysis*. Reading, MA: Addison-Wesley.

Rain, K. (1979). The decision to (not) buy a breakfast contract at Northwestern University. Mimeo.

Rhoades, R., Booth, R., Shaw, R., & Werge, R. (1982). Interdisciplinary development and transfer of postharvest technology at the International Potato Center. *The Role of Anthropologists and Other Social Scientists in Interdisciplinary Teams Developing Improved Food Production Technology*. Los Banos, Laguna, The Philippines: The International Rice Research Institute.

Rosenfeld, R. (1981). Academic men's and women's career mobility. *Social Science Research 10*, 337-363.

Roumasset, J. (1976). *Rice and Risk: Decision-Making Among Low Income Farmers*. Amsterdam: North Holland.

Roumasset, J., Boussard, J. M., & Singh, I. (1979). *Risk, Uncertainty, and Agricultural Development*. New York: Agricultural Development Council.

Roy, A. D. (1952). Safety first and the holding of assets. *Econometrica 20*(3), 431-449.

Schank, R., & Abelson, R. (1977). *Scripts, Plans, Goals and Understanding*. New York: Wiley and Sons.

Schoemaker, P. (1982). The expected utility model: Its variants, purposes, evidence, and limitations. *Journal of Economic Literature 20*, 529-563.

Schoepfle, M., Burton, M., & Morgan, F. (1984). Navajos and energy development: Economic decision making under political uncertainty. *Human Organization 43*(3), 265-276.

Spradley, J. (1979). *The Ethnographic Interview*. New York: Holt, Rinehart, and Winston.

Spradley, J. (1980). *Participant Observation*. New York: Holt, Rinehart, and Winston.

Tversky, A. (1972). Elimination by aspects: A theory of choice. *Psychological Review 28*, 1-39.

Tversky, A., & Kahneman, D. (1981). The framing of decisions and the psychology of choice. *Science 211*, 453-458.

Young, J. C. (1980). A model of illness treatment decisions in a Tarascan town. *American Ethnologist 7*(1), 106-131.

Young, J. C. (1981). *Medical Choice in a Mexican Village.* New Brunswick, NJ: Rutgers University Press.

Werner, O., & Schoepfle, G. M. (1987). *Systematic Fieldwork,* Vol 1 and 2. Newbury Park, CA: Sage.

Zabawa, R. (1984). The transformation of farming in Gadsden County, North Florida. Unpublished doctoral dissertation, Northwestern University.

ABOUT THE AUTHOR

CHRISTINA H. GLADWIN is currently an Associate Professor in the Food and Resource Economics Department, Institute of Food and Agricultural Sciences, University of Florida, Gainesville. She is also affiliated with the Anthropology department and Centers for African and Latin American Studies. She has a B.A. in physics from Catholic University, Washington, D.C. (1964), a Ph.D. in agricultural economics from the Food Research Institute, Stanford University (1978), and has also studied in the School of Social Sciences, U.C. Irvine (1969-71). She has done fieldwork and studied the decision making processes of small-scale producers and marketeers in Ghana (1967-68), Mexico (1973-74), Guatamala (1977-79), Malawi (1987), and north Florida (1980-89). Her research is a blend of anthropology and economics. Her current interests include the changing structure of United States agriculture, the demise of the full-time family farm and the survival of the part-time family farm; the role of women on the family farm and the increase in women's farming in industrial agricultures; the cognitive relationship between norms, plans, and decision processes; and large-scale shifts in norms and choice behavior.